Great Reefs
OF THE WORLD

Carl Roessler

Pisces Books
A division of Gulf Publishing Company
Houston, Texas

Great Reefs
OF THE WORLD

Pisces Books
A division of Gulf Publishing Company
P.O. Box 2608 □ Houston, Texas 77252-2608

10 9 8 7 6 5 4 3 2 1

ISBN 1-55992-058-0

Library of Congress Catalog Card Number: 92-072701

Printed in Hong Kong

Contents

Foreword

$\mathcal{T}$he Dream is the same, all across the tropical world. A mighty sun pours light upon the surface of a placid blue sea. Where the light falls upon coral reefs, spectacular hieroglyphics of aquamarine appear, beckoning to human explorers. Beneath the limpid surface, water of crystal clarity reveals mountainous ramparts of coral. These are the cathedrals of the sea, whose epic scale inspires us to awe and wonder.

From abyssal depths to sun-warmed shallows, the world's coral reefs offer us mosaics of complex life, lush color and endless intricacy. The number of coral reefs is great, and it would seem they should supply endless diving riches. The truth is more mundane: there are certain sites which are sublime, while many others are at best routine.

Over the years, one after another of these reef complexes have come within the reach of divers. The best have become enshrined in an unofficial pantheon, passed among divers by word of mouth. New divers soon learn that tropical resorts may offer reefs that are convenient but not very good; information about the world's remote and genuinely spectacular reefs helps these divers avoid wasted vacations.

After a lifetime of seeking out superior and even sublime reefs, and offering them to divers through my own company, I am intimately familiar with the Olympian sites — and how they differ from the rest. By sharing them I hope they will be forever preserved, and known for the precious, wild places they are.

With luck, the march of civilization will spare the treasures in this volume. In their unspoiled beauty and complexity, they offer divers serenity in an often hostile world.

◀ *Vertical precipices can be riotously colorful interruptions of the sea's endless blue.*

Introduction

*I*t was only 50 years ago that the first modern diving adventurer, Hans Hass, roamed the undersea world! Sailing his yacht *Xarifa* through the Red Sea and Indian Ocean, Hass made theatrical films that inspired young dreamers such as me.

Twenty years later, the French legend Jacques-Yves Cousteau followed Hass' voyages and expanded on them because of a crucial new ingredient—television. Suddenly, a broader audience could share in the undersea world, and sponsors would pay to reach that audience. Cousteau became an icon, and the modern sport of diving was born.

By 1950, Cousteau's demand regulator brought the use of scuba tanks for diving to America. At that time there was a small community of free-diving spearfishermen; most were young and could afford only fins, mask, snorkel, and speargun. The problem with spearing is that it is *selective*. It removes from the breeding stock the best and strongest individuals. Back then, however, none of us knew that our

◀ The "flowers" of the coral reef take many forms. This is the egg ribbon of a Spanish dancer nudibranch.

efforts could have any effect on the reef population. In blissful ignorance, young divers trained themselves to pierce the sea's modest defenses and attack its leading citizens.

By the late 1960s, underwater camera equipment largely replaced the speargun. Underwater photography gave us all the elements of hunting, stalking, and the moment of the kill, yet spared the prey. Indeed, pictures of fish by now have outlived their original subjects by many years.

Dive travel as a concept was virtually unknown in the 1950s and early 60s. Our diving was done on wrecks off New Jersey, or rocky islands off the California coast, or in the Florida Keys. The idea of following Hass or Cousteau to the far limits of the planet was still but a dream.

In 1964, I dove the reefs off the south coast of Puerto Rico and in 1965, with an ex-U.D.T. frogman, dove the Virgin Islands. I would hate to guess how few clients these destinations had at the time, but the idea of a vacation specifically to go diving slowly took hold.

In 1969, after a decade in the then-infant computer industry, I decided to move to the Caribbean and go into the practically nonexistent dive travel industry. Those were days when all of Bonaire could muster only seven tanks, and they were nothing to write home about. How could we build a destination for vacationing divers?

It turned out that the ingredients were there. Vacationers were offered a spartan bungalow, with breakfast and dinner in the "resort's" dining room. For diving, I would charter a local fishing boat, with its (usually colorful) captain. Add the tanks I had by then imported, and a minimalist box lunch: the dive travel "industry" had a new destination.

Similar efforts were taking place in the Bahamas, Cozumel, Hawaii, and Cayman Islands, and of course the Mediterranean, Red Sea, and Australia.

Perhaps the most important consequence of the movement toward dive vacations was the concomitant decline of spearing on the reefs. Spearing had inflicted noticeable damage; catches had declined, and even the most skilled practitioner returned with smaller fish in sparse numbers. By the time I took up residence in the Netherlands Antilles in 1969, the spearmen with whom I roamed already complained of declining catches. Strangely, they seemed never to realize that the lack of larger fish stemmed from their own depredations.

As biologists took up diving, their observations made the connection between spearfishing and the absence of larger fish; worse, they told us that in key species *only* the larger males (called supermales) were capable of breeding. Reef conservation was born, and underwater photography became the mainspring of diving.

Simultaneously, divers began to trade weekend diving near home for annual pilgrimages to warm, clear tropical waters.

What caused that shift was the realization that to dive near home we would spend several hours in our cars, then rent a boat and spend an hour or two getting to a dive site. A quick half-hour in cold, often murky New England water and we went through it all again to get home. Sometimes a fourteen-hour day was required to enjoy that half-hour in the water; even the most die-hard of us sensed this was a disproportionate return on our efforts.

When I went to the Caribbean for the first time I realized there was an alternative: by diving several times each day, a tropical diving vacation could yield more good diving than an entire season at home. The stage was set for divers to use the tropics for nearly all their diving. Today an entire industry has evolved to serve that need; many of today's divers own only the equipment with which to travel to the tropics. They do not even own scuba tanks and lead weights, for example. Those items are provided at any well-organized tropical destination.

This new structure of diving as a part of international travel has had one more salutary effect. Diving with minimal equipment in warm, clear water has extended the active diving career of most divers: rather than fight cold American, Canadian, or European waters, divers enjoy the spa-like water around the Equator.

Yet another positive consequence is that travelling divers become conservationists in the most positive sense of the word. Coming face to face with the marine creatures on healthy, undamaged reefs spurs divers to support efforts to protect those reefs. In the most extreme example of this, we are even seeing support among Australians to protect the much-maligned great white shark. Given this shark's media-generated "monster" image, such good sense shows that the roots of conservation run deep in all of us if only they can be tapped.

Finally, travelling divers become more skilled as divers and as underwater photographers than their stay-at-home confreres. By diving intensely (up to four or more scuba tanks each day) during their tropical sojourns, these travel-

Like some massive ghost, a great white shark Carcharias carcharodon *emerges from the ocean twilight.* ▶

In certain areas, modest currents garland coral pinnacles with magnificent carpets of color. These areas tend to be very remote.

ling divers improve at a startling pace. After all, intense training in any sport yields a quick building of skills, and tropical diving is structured for precisely that type of feedback loop.

While these comments make it clear that I am an enthusiastic supporter of tropical travel for divers, there is a dark

The great reefs of the tropics project a richness and grandeur uniquely their own. ▶

(Following page) *Clownfish* Amphiprion perideraion *shelter amid the poison-armed tentacles of an anemone. The clownfish secrete a skin mucous which prevents the lethal tentacles from harming them.*

side. Some of the world's best dive sites of twenty years ago have been severely impacted by crowds of avid divers. After all, sand kicked on corals by conservationists does just as much harm as that kicked by the unconcerned . . .

And so, with regret, I realize that some famous dive Meccas have been sacrificed to the mass-market segment of the sport. Without specifying, those of you who are divers can think of the most famous destinations of the past twenty years and suspect that they are damaged. This is particularly true if the famous diving is concentrated on one reef off the coast of a single island that has a "Hotel Row" capable of accommodating dozens or hundreds of divers.

Has such sacrifice been worth it? I believe so, because the legion of divers now dedicated to saving reefs will be a powerful force; the reefs we have lost were sacrificed, I hope, to that higher purpose. While perfection is impossible to obtain, a crusade of this kind will draw the attention of even the most obtuse.

To all new divers I urge care and consideration: use good technique, be thoughtful about the harm you might do to marine creatures, have experienced divers show you how to avoid inflicting damage—then enjoy the most luminous moments on our water-dominated planet.

Now to the adventure of international tropical diving . . .

The Caribbean and Bahamas

$\mathcal{A}$pproaching the task of describing the world's greatest diving sites requires a decision about sequence. Which areas, in what sequence, are included? Some divers may read significance into a sequence when I intend none.

I have begun where many divers begin their careers, in the Caribbean and Bahamas, and then worked outward to destinations such as Costa Rica, the Galapagos, and Hawaii.

The next and major segment will be the Pacific, with Micronesia and the Philippines in the central area, Fiji, the Solomons, Australia, Vanuatu, New Caledonia, and Papua New Guinea among our highlights. We will travel the Indian Ocean to visit the Maldives and Thailand. Then we'll finish with the sublime Red Sea.

The Caribbean

In the movement of continents that has taken place over the past 350 million years, the earth is believed to have evolved from a single continent amid a single sea. During that process, continental masses migrated across the globe, oceans were formed, mountains rose.

Among the seas formed, the Caribbean Basin is one of the most isolated. On its western boundary is the land bridge called Central America; on the eastern side the cold waters of the Atlantic Ocean form an equally complete barrier against the migration of tropical marine species.

Given complete isolation over the past million years, it is no surprise that Caribbean species are different from those of other seas. There are the same genera (butterflyfish, angelfish, groupers, snappers, et al.) but the representatives of each genus are unique to the Caribbean.

From the diver's perspective this means that with few exceptions, you see the same species of corals and fish from the Bahamas in the north to Bonaire in the south. What then would make one island or region possess better diving than another? Two factors predominate: the natural undersea topography, and human pressure.

The natural undersea topography of the Caribbean's greatest dive sites is unvarying: islands or remote reefs too small to have rivers or significant weather systems, and which are the mere exposed tops of sheer undersea mountains rising up out of deep, clear water.

A pair of royal grammas Gramma loreto *perform their perpetual dance for plankton against the background of tube sponges.*

◄ *Through a chasm in a massive reef, distant divers fly in inner space.*

Human pressure takes at least three forms: fishing, diving, and development. Over the years, many reefs near towns or villages have endured heavy fishing pressure. Now, some favored or well publicized islands are suffering from large numbers of divers impacting the same reefs day after day. Hotel-building has also altered the shorelines, interior bays, and reef ecology at certain islands.

All of this makes the Caribbean a place for careful choices. Some travellers will prefer diving out of well-developed centers such as Grand Cayman, Cozumel, or the Virgin Islands; others will purposely seek out unspoiled,

pristine, and therefore remote places such as Belize's Lighthouse Reef, Mexico's Chinchorro Banks, the Bahamas' Conception Island, or the Aves and Los Roques Islands off Venezuela.

Having specified a spectrum of choices, we may survey the Bahamas and Caribbean with them in mind.

The Bahamas

Diving in the Bahamas is very uneven. In the western Bahamas there has been significant reef damage due to destructive fishing with chemical agents, such as Clorox. Yet sites around the Tongue of the Ocean, a 13,000-foot-deep chasm between Nassau and Andros Island, can still be superb. Further down the chain, Conception Island is practically untouched after all these years. For the potential traveller, a bit of careful research or advice from experts could be crucial. It might make the difference between diving on quite impressive reefs or on barren graveyards.

When I dove on reefs out of Freeport, I was unpleasantly surprised at the scale of the damage I saw. While the reef contours were quite dramatic, and led to a plunging dropoff to ocean depths, the entire surface of the reef had been killed. Overlain with a layer of smothering algae, it hosted almost no fish. So, when I invoke the specter of bad diving, it is depressingly real.

Yet other areas are lively and healthy, particularly from the zone of Nassau (New Providence Island) and Andros to the southernmost islands.

Nassau is a major hub for incoming services, but many of the southern islands are still undeveloped. If you get off the beaten track you will still find reefs with swaying, bush-like gorgonians, soft, fluid anemones, and dropoffs whose walls are still covered with marine life.

3

The real message, then, is that there is world-class diving in the Bahamas, but it is seen by taking your vacation on live-aboard dive boats which go to the remote areas. This tautology is the primal law of dive travel all over the world: if you want to see the best diving, a live-aboard dive vessel is more likely to deliver it.

In the Caribbean Basin, such vessels operate in the Bahamas, Turks and Caicos (which lie just south of the Bahamas), Cayman Islands, Belize, the Bay Islands of Honduras, the Netherlands Antilles, St. Maarten/Saba, and the Aves and Roques Islands off Venezuela.

In addition, of course, a host of shore-based resorts crowd islands such as the Caymans and Cozumel, while lesser concentrations carpet the entire spectrum of Caribbean Islands.

The Turks and Caicos Islands

The southernmost islands of the Bahamas chain are separated only by political jurisdiction; the resulting island nation is known as the Turks and Caicos Islands. The two distinct island groups are the Turks, a string of small islands running north and south, and a large plateau with scattered islands known as the Caicos. Between the two island groups is a deep channel frequented by migrating whales, the Caicos Channel.

Diving in the Turks and Caicos is surprisingly similar to diving in Bonaire, which lies near the coast of Venezuela, far to the south. This illustrates the essential unity of the Caribbean Basin. Here are two distinct locales at opposite ends of the Caribbean which are almost twinned in physical terms: long, gently sloping shallows off the beach which are

◀ *A trumpetfish* Aulastomus maculatus *sometimes hunts by hiding itself close to the body of another fish, in this case a tiger grouper* Mycteroperca tigris.

The reef's citizens wear impressive finery. This is the golden grouper Cephalopholis fulva.

excellent for snorkeling, then a dropoff which is usually sloping but occasionally steep. Even the fish species—goatfish in placid schools, paired butterflyfish, solitary barracuda—elicited déjà vu for me since I had lived years ago in Bonaire.

The Virgin Islands

Moving southward from the Turks and Caicos we enter the Caribbean proper. The islands of the Caribbean are independent tiny nations, or are affiliated with major countries. The Cayman Islands, for example, have long been part of the British commonwealth, while Guadeloupe and Martinique are actually districts of France. The American islands of the Caribbean are the U. S. Virgin Islands, which lie just to the east of Puerto Rico, itself a possible future

state of the United States. Some of the Virgin Islands have historically been administered by Great Britain, and are consequently known as the British Virgin Islands. American divers hardly note the political distinction, moving freely amid both groups by boat, ferry, and commuter plane.

The British Virgins are known for the famed wreck of the *Rhone*, on which legions of divers and snorkelers have made their earliest excursions. Other scattered dive sites are noteworthy for stands of the broadleaf elkhorn coral *Acropora palmata*.

Divers who want plenty of development—hotels, shopping, and dining—are drawn to the Virgin Islands despite the undeniable fact that the diving here is not in the league of, say, Belize. The Virgins are well-suited to those who want some diving, but who also place a premium on other activities amid physically beautiful surroundings.

The Cayman Islands

This three-island group has developed explosively over the past decade, to the point where significant traffic jams gridlock the main streets at times. Twenty years ago, the Caymans were a low-key paradise; now they host massive hotel facilities and a dive boat fleet that resembles nothing so much as a naval armada. Boats make advance arrangements to avoid squabbles over moorings; this and other signs of overcrowding sometimes put off experienced divers. For new divers, however, the Caymans are one of the best places to start your diving travels.

There are big dropoffs all around the islands; the most famous sites are on the northern coasts of both Grand Cayman and Little Cayman. The Bloody Bay Wall at Little Cayman

◀ *A large rock hind* Epinephelus adsencionis *decides how close it will let the photographer approach before bolting.*

may be the best single dive site in the Caribbean. If it is not *the* best, it is one of a very short list of great Caribbean walls.

Over the years, the immensely greater numbers of divers have literally created one landmark dive site. Years ago we used to anchor just inside the northern bay of Grand Cayman; fishermen also used it as a protected anchorage. The water was only fifteen feet deep over an empty sand bottom.

The fishermen would clean their catches and throw the offal over the side. A few stingrays would be attracted by the free food, and scavenge a meal. When divers realized the stingrays could be attracted by food, diving with the rays became an everyday event. Now, dive boats vie for the anchorage and dozens of divers can be milling over the sandy terrain, reducing visibility. Still, the magic of the rays is undeniable. Sting Ray City has entered the pantheon of famous animal encounters for divers.

Still, the largest attraction of the Caymans are the steep undersea walls that surround the islands. By now, dive boats have enumerated literally hundreds of dive sites; eighty or ninety percent would be dominated by wall diving. There is undeniable magic for divers when they soar across a coral garden and suddenly the bottom drops away in a sheer precipice. Suddenly, the diver feels exalted, blessed with the power of flight . . .

Cozumel

For one who has travelled the Caribbean for twenty five years, the changes in places like Cozumel and the Caymans are unnerving. When I first visited Cozumel Island in 1967, there were three small beach resorts and a deserted coastline stretching away for miles to the south. At our anchorages on Palancar Reef, our converted native fishing boat would be the only vessel in sight, and the sandy shallows beneath our hull were filled with conch as far as the eye could see.

Those days, while vivid in memory, have receded into the echoing emptiness of time. Today, half of Texas is in Cozumel for each weekend diving package. Hotels line the beach, and diveboats are anchored in a marine parking lot above the mile-long reef-segment called Palancar. No longer a place for the sophisticated explorer, Cozumel has become a place for crowds.

An interesting comparison: Palancar Reef is a mammoth, Grand Canyon-like experience, with caverns, canyons, tunnels and other topography on an immense scale. That means that even the damage inflicted by thousands of divers has merely destroyed the surface of the vast structure. New divers in particular are still digesting the space-walking experience of diving, and have not yet settled down to search out individual reef citizens. For them this colossal sepulchre can still be a magic place simply because of its immense physical form.

The comparison is this: Palancar's physical size and structure is still an attraction though its corals and fish have been decimated. Other Caribbean sites are not so fortunate. When their reefs decline so, too, does their attractiveness in the marketplace.

Bonaire and Curaçao

Bonaire and Curaçao in the Netherlands Antilles offer a real contrast to Cozumel. There are dropoffs around each island, but they tend to be modest and sloping. Lacking vertical drama, the diving naturally is more dependent upon the health of its coral gardens. Here the inevitable damage inflicted by divers can be crucial.

Cleaner wrasse and shrimp pick parasites from the face of a young Nassau grouper Epinephelus striatus.

A cleaner shrimp Stenopus hispidus *perches atop an iridescent sponge.* ▶

(Previous left) Jessica Roessler explores a reef wall bedecked with colorful sponges.

(Previous right) A blackcap basslet Gramma melacara *is seen against the radiant backdrop of a tube sponge.*

In recent years, corals have been killed by sustained higher water temperatures; in addition, the natural wear and tear inflicted by thousands of divers at any successful tourist island becomes increasingly evident. Still, at the northwestern coast of Bonaire there are dramatic coral gardens and walls which have been saved up to now only by their distance from the hotels. My personal hope is that diver traffic will not reach to the point of damaging those last pristine reefs in the Antilles. When I lived there, years ago, these were my personal favorites; I see them now in my imagination as they were then, and hope that they may endure.

Klein Curaçao, a tiny islet off the south coast of busy Curaçao, has also been spared visits from too many divers. It is weather dependent, in that the waves from strong winds wrap completely around the small island. In good weather, however, the walls around the island are prodigious. Huge barracudas and massive snappers in deeper sites can up the drama quotient substantially.

Roatan

Roatan and the other Bay Islands lie off the northern coast of Honduras. There are some excellent dropoffs here, and shallow coral fields of considerable beauty. Over the years the reef fish have been thinned out by an active fishing community, but at their best, dive sites in the Bay Islands can rival those of Belize or the Caymans.

Belize

Belize has recently become a Mecca for those Caribbean divers who prefer live-aboard dive cruisers. That is simply because Belize's best sites lie up to sixty miles off the coast, at remote Lighthouse Reef.

Dives at the prime anchorages at Lighthouse Reef are very instructive about the effect of man on the entire Caribbean Sea. The visiting diver will see live conch, healthy Nassau groupers, and large snappers, while overhead may wheel a hundred horse-eye jacks.

Since all of these spots are prime targets for fishermen, their continued presence tells us that their distance from fishing villages has protected them. To the experienced diver the thought immediately occurs that a few decades ago the entire Caribbean was like this. When I first dived Belize years ago, perhaps 100–200 divers would see these reefs in a year. Today the number is closer to 2,000, with dark implications for divers who visit some years from now.

Today, however, all of these islands beckon divers and introduce them to the sport. Once these (often neophyte) divers have seen clear, warm-water diving, the reefs of the entire world beckon.

Given those capsule summaries of some leading destinations, how does one choose the best Caribbean diving? A few guideposts:

1. Islands which are the tops of undersea mountains rising from open sea usually have big dropoffs, and will usually have clear water. Examples are the Caymans, Cozumel, and Bonaire.
2. Island *groups*, such as the Virgin Islands and Grenadines, often sit atop huge undersea plateaus. In

A juvenile queen triggerfish Balistes vetula *spends its pelagic phase hidden in floating sargassum weed.* ▶

these plateau formations we can encounter turbid water conditions; this is because the open sea water does not circulate efficiently over the plateau among the islands. The islands then act as baffles to current flows, trapping turbid water among them.

3. Places *without* hotel development, such as the Aves and Roques Islands, Lighthouse Reef (Belize), Conception Island (Bahamas), and Chinchorro Banks (Mexico), often have the healthiest reefs. It is simply a matter of accessibility and traffic damage. The more divers, the more damage. The unknown, undeveloped places are often the best treasures. This is a theme which will be at the heart of our later travels in the remote areas of the Pacific and Red Sea.

Again, how then does a diver choose? That depends on how important *diving* is to his or her vacation.

For those to whom the diving comes *first*, a live-aboard cruise to an undeveloped reef is the best choice. This is purely and simply because live-aboards go to reefs that are beyond the reach of the hotel day boats. The reefs the live-aboards seek out are thus subjected to much less diver-inflicted damage. These undamaged reefs support a richer fauna, and give us more of those wonderful animal/human interactions that are the heart and soul of diving.

Those who want the "bright lights"—shopping, casinos, restaurants—will choose the heavily developed islands and pay the price in diving that endures heavy traffic.

The third alternative is the "away from it all" shore resort—some tiny bungalows on a remote island with

◄ *A young black grouper* Mycteroperca bonaci *pauses before fleeing, not realizing that the pause was enough to capture the moment.*

limited facilities. The diving may be good but must be within a few miles of the resort to be reached with a day boat. These tiny resorts are an attempt to mimic what a live-aboard cruiser offers while still basing on shore. Like a live-aboard, a tiny resort deals with smaller numbers of divers and inflicts less damage on local reefs. However, the diving offered is still in a limited radius around the hotel site.

At its best, the Caribbean reefs offer dives which could be symbolized by two locations: the north walls of Grand Cayman and Little Cayman, where sheer precipices plunge dramatically downward for thousands of feet, and the remote reefs of Belize, alive with fish because they are too far out for day boat fishermen to reach. For me, these two areas are the archetypes. Other areas resemble these to a greater or lesser extent. Places such as Cozumel, the Aves, Roatan and the other Bay Islands, and Andros and Conception in the Bahamas, come close to the vertical wall configuration of the Caymans. Places such as Bonaire, the Virgin Islands, and Chinchorro Banks have less drama vertically but often pleasant sun-drenched expanses of coral garden.

Finally, there is what I call "compared to what?" A new diver on his or her first visit to the Caribbean has no ability to judge the quality of the diving. It may be pretty beaten up, but clear water, sunshine and the feel of flying will thrill that diver and he/she will declare it sensational. It is only later when the more experienced diver looks closely at the reef that he or she sees damage and blight. It is at that point that the choices I have outlined above suddenly become meaningful to that diver.

For these new divers I have good news: if you like the Caribbean's best diving, there are at least twenty-five more "Caribbeans" scattered around the tropical world. The Caribbean is but the first rung of a ladder that "takes you to the stars" . . .

The Eastern Pacific

One of the most interesting areas for divers during the past decade has been the Eastern Pacific. Long dismissed as a "dead zone" compared to the color-filled and glamorous South Pacific, the east had its partisans but their voices were seldom heard.

Then, abruptly, destinations such as Cocos Island, Socorro, San Benedicto, and the northern islands of the Galapagos were the hottest news in diving. Hammerhead sharks, manta rays, whale sharks, and massive schools of open water fish made these remote sites Mecca for a hardy but growing segment of the diving public.

Baja California

Historically, Baja California's La Paz had filled this niche for thrill seekers. However, a quarter century of fishing, diving and uneven dive services left Baja vulnerable. When pioneering divers returned from Cocos Island, Socorro, and the islands of Wolf and Wenman in the Galapagos with thrilling

◄ *The white-striped, or king angelfish* Holocanthus passer, *graces Baja's waters; its range also includes the Galapagos and Cocos Island.*

tales, the adventurous reacted swiftly. Baja began to decline in prominence. When diving with pelagics was a topic of conversation, Baja was spoken of in the past tense. New champions were crowned. An era ended.

In its glory days, Baja's Sea of Cortez was dominated by tales of big animals at the famed seamounts. Divers would drop into currents, descend to 50–80 feet and drift toward the seamounts. Visibility averaged 60–80 feet, and the fortunate were rewarded by drifting into schools of hammerhead sharks, or by encounters with huge manta rays.

The manta ray sightings ended, and word spread that local fishermen had killed them. Divers returned less excited than in former years. There are still big animal adventures in the Sea of Cortez, but the frequency of those sightings has declined.

Meanwhile, travellers to the Galapagos, Cocos Island, and Socorro began telling tales of their early voyages. These accounts sounded like the glory days of Baja—hammerheads by the hundred, mantas, even whale sharks.

Suddenly, people wanted to go to these new pelagic arenas.

It must immediately be said that these islands are desperately remote and undeveloped; that is precisely the reason that large marine creatures may still be found there. There are no airports, tourist hotels, and sandy beaches. Instead,

forbidding cliffs of volcanic rock tower above gray seas roiled by swift currents. These deep ocean currents cause upwellings of nutrient-rich water around the lonely outposts. The resulting hearty soup of plankton supports a massive food chain. Vast schools of jacks, creole fish, anchovy, mullet, herring, chub, and rainbow runner swarm in the food-laden water only to be preyed upon by larger creatures. Hammerhead sharks, Galapagos sharks, whale sharks, and manta rays are found with sufficient regularity to inspire a small subset of travelling divers to seek them out with fanatic devotion.

An interesting aspect of these big animal sites is that they are the very antithesis of the kinds of destinations divers sought during prior decades. In earlier times, divers sought warm, crystal clear, tropical waters with sandy beaches, palm trees, and calm weather; rich reefs with a variety of colorful animals were sine qua non—and most divers wanted, at most, an occasional shark. In truth, this dream structure was an echo of the early days of diving, when sharks were thought to be savage monsters.

Cocos Island

Now see how the pendulum has swung. As I sit writing this I am at anchor off Cocos Island. Cocos, (also known as *Isla del Coco*) lies in the Inter-Tropical Convergence Zone, some 270 miles southwest of Puntarenas, Costa Rica. This island of 14 square miles receives some twenty-seven *feet* of rainfall each year; towering waterfalls punctuate its outer perimeter of 300-foot-high sheer walls. Clouds churn over its higher elevations, while green moss and lush vegetation festoon the plunging battlements. Rain comes swiftly and often.

◀ *Omnipresent sea lions cavort off the bouldered bottom at Baja's dive sites.*

A pair of Mexican air force fighter planes zoom in above a rocky islet, adding zest to the diving day.

All along the flanks of Cocos, waterfalls rain down from the interior highlands where up to 400 inches of rain fall annually.

In the vast, open waters off Cocos Island, great squadrons of hammerhead sharks Sphyrna lewini *ghost by.*

◄ *Marbled rays* Myliobatis *swarm over a barren sea floor; their placid gatherings suggest socializing rather than breeding or defense.*

Occasionally a solitary hammerhead will swim right up to a diver; I suspect poor eyesight, because the sharks register the diver's presence by bolting in fear.

However lovely and evocative the tall cliffs and misting rains of this isolated island, Cocos' dive sites are what justifies our long cruise and lonely sojourn. Off the coast are scattered small rocky islets. Underwater, their tumbled boulders plunge down into darkness in water whose visibility may be from 30–75 feet. At about 100 feet you enter a thermocline (marked visually by a mixing layer in which the water looks oily) where the temperature abruptly drops by 5–10 degrees. Beneath this barrier the deep water is dark but crystal clear, to abyssal depths.

To understand the profound shift divers here have made from classic tropical dive experiences, imagine this: you have jumped from a boat into water near a wave-washed pinnacle, and descended 100 feet. Now you drift along in a current, in the darkness, with no idea where the sea will take you. In the vast gloom huge flights of hammerhead sharks can often be seen; sailfish, mantas, even whale sharks are only a matter of sufficient luck and time in the water. They all pass here, in a bouillabaisse of swarming creole wrasse, rainbow runners, needlefish and other nervous bait schools. You drift at various depths for up to 40 minutes, enjoying whatever creatures emerge from the enveloping darkness.

Toward the end of the dive, you rise to the surface perhaps a half-mile or more from the islet. Dusky sharks may be escorting you by now, and as you drift on the surface they become quite attentive. You signal, and a speedboat picks you up. This is indeed a far cry from diving the sun-splashed coral shallows of the South Pacific.

(Previous left) *Cocos is filled with life: healthy schools of barred soldierfish* Myripristis, *goatfish* Mulloidichthys, *and horse-eyed jack* Caranx. *The jacks around Manuelita Island form a school so dense it looks like an undersea mountain.*

(Previous right) *Cocos' rocky islets are honeycombed with caverns offering shelter from predation to a wide variety of fish species.*

The horizon is ringed with massive volcanoes, yet Tagus Cove seems a haven of ethereal peace.

The Galapagos

Except for the humidity and rainfall on the island, much of the foregoing would also describe diving Wolf and Wenman Islands in the northern Galapagos. Those outposts, some 300 miles south of Cocos Island, as well as Socorro/San

A diver regards the typical Galapagos substrate—lava rock overlain with barnacles and encrusting sponge. ▶

Benedicto 300 miles to the north are dry and barren because they lie outside the Convergence Zone.

What all three destinations share absolutely is utter loneliness, a volcanic origin, powerful boulder-strewn underwater vistas and big animals in open water. No colorful coral reef, no crystal-clear visibility, just the thrill of conquering your own fears . . .

These three regions add an important new dimension to diving. Places such as the Caribbean have long offered pretty reefs with almost no big animal encounters that might frighten new divers. Most divers did their early travel to these destinations, whose placidity helped potential divers overcome their initial apprehension. After a number of Caribbean dives, even the timid have built reasonable confidence. Many South Pacific and Red Sea sites add literally hundreds of beautiful species to a diver's experience. The next step is an occasional encounter with larger marine creatures in clear water conditions. With the visibility excellent, divers soon see that the pelagic creatures are no threat.

Some of my favorite places such as the Sudan, Papua New Guinea, and Australia's Coral Sea add relatively frequent encounters with sharks, rays, and turtles in crystal water to spice the beauty of coral reefs. Now the Cocos, Wolf/Wenman, and Socorro/San Benedicto experiences add a rugged new area totally unlike all others. Forsaking coral and color, undersea adventurers leap into swift currents and murky water for the adrenaline surge of the unpredictable, even vaguely sinister, experience. This is *not* dangerous diving, but there is the thrill of the unexpected in a setting redolent of our most ancient fears—meeting the unknown at the edge of darkness.

The Galapagos Islands have been famous since Charles Darwin's explorations for their population of endemic

species. Walks on the various islands reveal a cornucopia of unique species—finches, doves, iguanas, tortoises, and other creatures which evolved from their ancestors in a biological hothouse devoid of competition. This unusual condition occurred because the islands erupted volcanically from the sea five to fifteen million years ago, utterly devoid of life. Over the centuries they were populated by survivors on driftwood borne from mainland South America by the Humboldt Current. So isolated were these islands and so uncomplicated their environment that tortoises and finches, for example, evolved as separate species by directly adapting to the foliage of each separate island they inhabited.

In the green, cool waters of the Humboldt, inshore marine species, current-borne from Baja or South America, evolved as well. Subspecies of sea lion, marbled grouper, and surgeonfish are among the nearly one-third of inshore species that are endemic. Every time a photographer points a camera above or below the water, there is a 30% chance or more that the subject is unique to these islands. With luck, the observant diver may even see the elusive wrasse-assed bass, dive with penguins, or observe cormorants (fishing birds) hunting for fish thirty feet below the surface.

Socorro and San Benedicto Islands boast an endemic angelfish called the Clarion angelfish; nature's fecundity spawns species for every unoccupied niche, it seems. For divers, that is the glory of exploring remote dive sites. Like birdwatchers, many divers and photographers "collect" sightings (or photographs) of species. During the cold days of winter ashore, these memories from the sea sustain us . . .

◄ *The rocky crevices are filled with eels of various species who are ready to challenge us at any time.*

In a peaceful cove, a massive bull sea lion Zalophus *roars in on the human intruder at top speed to protect the female sea lions or his turf.*

At James Island, rocky grottoes are filled with diminutive, playful fur sea lions.

(Previous left) *The Galapagos tartan hawkfish* Oxycirrhites *was never known until one of my photos of it was published in a magazine.*

(Previous right) *Schooling lemon butterflyfish* Chaetodon miliaris *swarm on the flanks of a volcanic crater.*

◀ *On the ceiling of a cave (note flattened air bubbles!) a nudibranch* Notodoris *browses on encrusting sponges in gaudy colors.*

During a night dive, a crab pauses in its dainty feeding to see whether the photographer will move on.

Hawaii

The Hawaiian Islands are another set of once-remote volcanic mountains formed by a hotspot under the earth's crust punching lava through a series of crustal ruptures. Like the Galapagos or Cocos, these pristine islands were seeded by currents. Unlike those other outposts, the Hawaiian Islands were at the end of a long circuit of current which subjected tropical South Pacific larvae to arctic temperatures. As a result, Hawaii's coral and fish variety is small compared to other tropical Pacific islands. Moreover, its relatively clear waters will not support the immense biota of Cocos or the Galapagos. Thus, Hawaiian diving tends to be the playground of the inexperienced, while more sophisticated divers fly right on through to Fiji, Truk Lagoon and other spectaculars of the central and southern Pacific. As a point of comparison, Hawaii has some 850 species of fish, while Australia boasts 2,300, and the Philippines nearly 2,800.

One important consideration for divers in the Hawaiian Islands is the paucity of corals. Divers moving westward from the Caribbean diving are often disappointed at the lack of corals, finding themselves instead in a severe moonscape of black lava rock. While the lava forms arches and caverns that make interesting dives, its lack of color and variety put it at a disadvantage compared to other zones.

Hawaii's best diving is in the open blue water around the islands. Here, in water thousands of feet deep, divers may see dolphins, pilot whales, bullfish, and pelagic sharks. It goes without saying that such diving is hardly for the novice or fainthearted. Many divers choose Hawaii each year despite its modest inshore diving, though more and more are using it as a brief way station to the Pacific. This could lead to stasis or even decline in guest-diver numbers.

On the other hand, the pelagic-oriented diving of Cocos Island, Socorro, and the northern Galapagos seem destined for as much growth as their limited facilities will allow. These successors to the Sea of Cortez represent an important new attraction to help diving grow. The thrill seeking audience will find that their diving offers a variety of adrenaline-charged moments.

Those who have drifted in green water a hundred feet below the surface and looked up through a squadron of hammerheads will never forget the experience. Will it keep us from wanting to dive the crystal waters of the Red Sea or Fiji? Of course not. It will merely feed our dreams to see all of the greatest sites.

Divers may now anticipate many years of exploring undersea wonders. From cathedrals of coral beneath sunlit seas to Stygian gloom populated by mysterious monsters, a lifetime of thrills await the explorer within us.

The Central Pacific

The Central Pacific is an immense area, dominated by the scattered islands of Micronesia. Twenty-one-hundred islands arise haphazardly across three million square miles of ocean, but their entire land area is smaller than the state of Connecticut.

For the past two decades, diving in Micronesia meant diving the sunken wrecks of the Japanese Fourth Fleet in Truk Lagoon, or diving the reefs off the 300 floating garden islands of Palau. These are genuine diving classics, destinations whose enshrinement in the pantheon of great diving is assured. For twenty years, Palau and Truk have been the first world-class Pacific islands divers have sought out.

Other Micronesian islands are now emerging as dive locales. While only time will tell whether any become as famous as Truk and Palau, it is fascinating to speculate how Micronesia's tapestry of undersea attractions may expand.

◄ *A clownfish* Amphiprion perideraion *challenges us from the safety of its host anemone's lethal arms.*

Micronesia

Palau

Palau's outer reef wall in the vicinity of Ngemelis Pass is the classic plunging dropoff. From just beneath the surface to a thousand feet and more in a straight vertical drop, it is one of the marine world's most awesome sights. Around the reef corner a mere mile to the south, two other legendary attractions are found.

The Blue Corner is an undersea projection of coral which is swept by currents. It is a gathering place for literally hundreds of barracuda, sharks, and other pelagic species, and yet a relatively easy dive. Its deeper slopes are punctuated by gorgonian fans and soft coral colonies in pink, purple, and yellow. When tidal currents are flowing, not only do all of these invertebrates extend their brilliant polyps, the blue waters above them teem with patrolling sharks, schooling barracuda, and other pelagic species. The total effect is stunning. Photographers rush about trying to capture the ineffable. It is better merely to pause, open your senses and simply absorb it.

▲ *From the air we see the true glory of Palau's garden islands.*

▲ *Every shallow bay is another visual delight.*

On a wall at 170 feet, brilliant gorgonians bloom in near-darkness. ▶

◀ *A diver soars beneath a towering coral wall at Ngemelis Pass, Palau.*

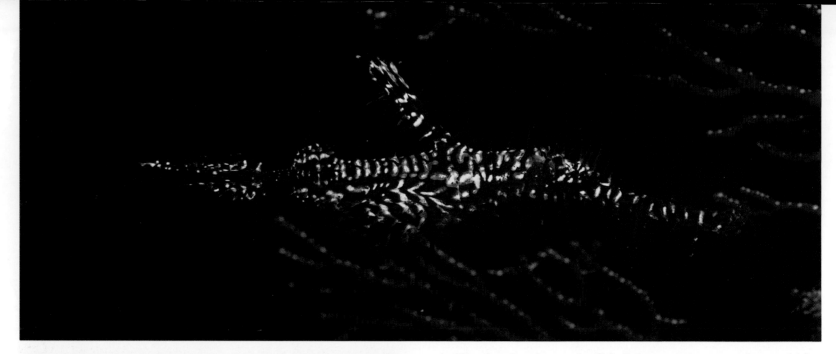

▲ *The lovely ghost pipefish* Solenostomus paradoxus *hides amid the arms of a gorgonian fan.*

◄ *Palau's coral walls are filled with outbursts of color such as these soft corals* Dendronephthya.

A bit further south along the reef is the quadruple Blue Hole, where four vertical tunnels pierce the reef and connect to an undersea cavern 110 feet from the surface. From the cavern you can swim beneath the entire outer reef wall and ascend to the surface up the crowded face of the coral precipice.

Dives such as these draw enthusiasts to Palau, despite the many airplane hours required to reach its remote location north of Darwin, Australia and south of Tokyo.

In twos and threes the manta rays approach us; sometimes up to ten will be at the cleaning station together.

Yap

As the prime example of how Micronesia's diving may expand, recently divers choosing Palau have begun adding three-day stops in Yap as part of their itinerary. Yap has limited but excellent diving facilities, and from November to May it has manta rays at a predictable location, the channel at M'il. Yap is a wonderful example of how the sport of diving grows. One sublime attraction can act as a magnet; its visitors then try other nearby islands which may bloom into their own prominence if they have some noteworthy feature such as the passes in Yap where the mantas gather.

Diving with the mantas of Yap is one of those experiences that spice even a lifetime of diving. Apparently the clear ocean waters that surround Yap have only a modest supply of the plankton upon which the mantas feed. Yet Yap's broad, sunbaked lagoon has a plentiful supply that supports a generous population of these great butterflies of the sea. Since the food supply is rich in the lagoon and relatively poor in the surrounding open water, it is really no surprise that the mantas are found in the lagoon.

In the center of one pass on the north side of the island is a large coral shelf. The placement of this reef structure funnels and concentrates the tidal flow. It is a natural feeding funnel for the rays; moreover, a number of cleaner wrasse have taken up residence on the structure. On any given day between November and May a diver can hover quietly just above the coral and soon be joined by several rays whose wingspans may reach eight to twelve feet.

The rays are initially cautious; the photographer must be patient. After a while the rays become quite comfortable with the human intruders. They will literally approach close enough to touch. I resist the impulse, for the magic of the moment should not be disturbed.

Soon mantas and humans share a graceful, slow-motion ballet of such ineffable beauty that its elements are burned into the mind for endless replay. This is a place, and an experience, unique in all my travels. Yet it does have powerful parallels to other sublime sites around the planet—the great white sharks of Dangerous Reef in South Australia, the rays of Grand Cayman's Sting Ray City, the groupers at the Cod Hole on the Great Barrier Reef, the sharks of Sha'ab Rumi in the Sudan, or their cousins at North Horn in the Coral Sea.

These and other gatherings of species provide human explorers with the stuff of dreams. Each place has an awesome symmetry that overwhelms the senses, ties the tongue. I had heard descriptions of Yap's Mantas and yet, when six huge rays hovered before me, my mind was somehow unprepared for them. Their majesty, their effortless grace, their gentle curiosity will always be with me.

There are the magic moments under tropic seas; those who experience them are forever changed . . .

Truk Lagoon

Truk Lagoon is another world-renowned destination with its own special attraction. As many as ninety sunken Japanese ships and aircraft are now pinpointed for diving, and a substantial proportion involve depths of no more than 70–80 feet. Massive freighters such as the *Shinkoku Maru*, *Rio de Janiero Maru*, *Fujikawa Maru*, *Sankisan Maru*, and *Heian Maru* have major superstructures within 10–40 feet of the surface.

It is true of course that other wrecks such as the *Seiko Maru*, *San Francisco Maru*, *Nippo Maru*, and more are 120 feet deep or more. However, publicity given to these deeper wrecks and the I-169 submarine at 90–130 feet have led many divers to believe that deep diving is required at Truk. Quite the opposite is true, and Truk has thrilled novices just as reliably as it has impressed the veterans.

The keys to Truk are three: the "space-walking" experience, the echo of conflict, and the marine life with which the sunken wrecks are wreathed.

When you soar down through the water on a day when it is clear, you feel like a bird in the sky, wheeling on invisible zephyrs. The engulfed freighters and supply ships are vast constants, immutable, while we are but transitory observers. Sometimes when I am home I marvel at the fact that the reefs and wrecks I love are always out there where I left them, as enduring as the stars.

◄ *The steel of the wrecks form a reef structure as complex and wonderfully rich as any in the world.*

In Yap, manta rays Manta birostis *gather at the M'il Channel to feed and to be cleaned.* ►

▲ *One hundred fifty-five feet below the surface, a battle tank sits forever mute on the deck of the* San Francisco Maru.

Truk's wrecks are immense, a fact best appreciated on days when the water is clear. ▶

A diver is dwarfed by the mast of the Nippo Maru.

A diver enters the bridge structure of the Fujikawa Maru.

(Previous left) Soft corals, algae, and hydrocorals bloom in utter profusion as mild currents bring them rich feeding.

(Previous right) Blue damselfish Dascyllus coeruleus *are framed by corals and sponges on the mast of the* Kansho Maru.

Aerial view of Truk Lagoon. In the scene lie probably twenty sunken wrecks.

(Below and right) Soft coral colonies seem astonishingly healthy and prolific on Truk's wrecks.

The profusion of corals seems only to increase with each new site. This is the Sankisan Maru.

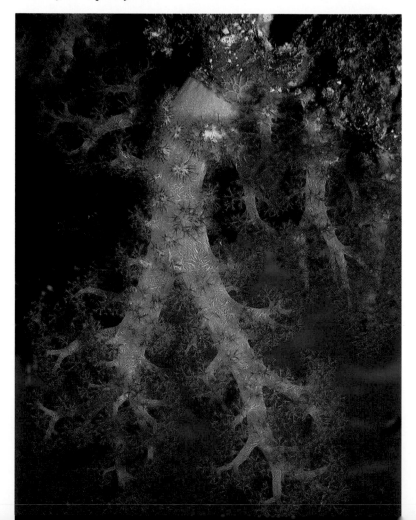

Wreck artifacts are found at all depths. Here, a diver mans the bow gun of the Dai Nhi Nho Maru.

◀ *A delicate hydrocoral colony grows on the steel of a sunken freighter.*

A davit of the Sankisan Maru *frames a diver with elegant corals.*

The artifacts of war, frozen in time.

No terrestrial garden can equal the richness of a Pacific coral reef.

On a smaller scale, certain of Truk's wrecks are riots of life. Their position in the meandering currents of the immense lagoon favor the *Shinkoku*, *Sankisan*, and *Fujikawa* Marus above all others. Despite significant diver traffic over a twenty-year period, they are still festooned with spectacular colonies of soft coral in hot colors. Other wrecks such as the *Nippo*, *Kansho*, *Fumatsuki*, *Unkai*, and *Rio de Janiero* offer powerful variations on the theme: clusters of hard and soft coral, nudibranchs, octopus, moray eels, and legions of colorful tropical fish soften and blur the hard outlines of war. Truk's diving is paradoxically some of the most restful and peaceful I know.

What makes Truk unique among all other wreck diving regions is the number and comparatively shallow depth of its wrecks. It is eminently possible during the unpredictable periods of clearer water for snorkelers or novice divers to be as awed and fulfilled by the scale of Truk's drowned monuments as experienced divers.

For all these reasons, Truk Lagoon's place in the Hall of Fame is assured.

The echo of conflict implicit in these darkling hulks draws World War II buffs powerfully, as well as that small percentage of divers for whom wreck diving is the *only* diving. On and in these sunken Japanese ships you find battle tanks, fighter planes, field guns, ammunition, and other detritus of war in postures as horrifically frozen as Picasso's *Geurnica* painting. We dive in a time warp, imagining the screams of attack planes, bombs, and men echoing into the unique silence of this monstrous tomb. We emerge elevated yet humbled, wondering what dark quirk of our species makes this horror inevitable every few decades . . .

Divers and snorkelers are dwarfed by the massive graphic elements of Truk's wrecks.

The Philippines

If there is any "hard-luck" destination in all of diving, it is these 7,000 beautiful islands.

Over many years I have done some of my most rewarding photography on remote reefs here; yet through the years I always felt the threat of a burgeoning Filipino population right behind me.

Two decades ago, the Philippines were noted for a singular blessing: their reefs contained more than 2,800 species of fish, a greater variety than anywhere else on earth. Their invertebrate life was equally prolific. The Philippines were simply one of the finest places on the planet for underwater photography.

Over the past decade, however, three powerful forces have darkened the horizon. A growing population has needed more food; this need inevitably led to destructive but quick

The rim of Tubbataha Reef is a tapestry of color and life.

On a shadowed wall, coral colonies bloom far from the placid surface.

fishing practices, and internal political upheavals have frightened away travelling divers.

From a narrow viewpoint, the real disaster was the fishing. Dynamite, Clorox bombs, and squads of children crushing the reef corals with stones to drive fish into nets claimed reef after reef. In a cruel paradox, the most remote reefs were most at risk because dynamiters could devastate at will out of sight of any protective authorities.

In the end, divers could never be sure that a reef they loved last year would not be rubble this year. So, the Philippines as an active dive destination went into decline. Famous sites such as Apo Reef were wiped out, others such as Tubbataha, Basterra, and Arena were cratered with their first dynamite explosions. The tragedy here is that these

◀ *A friendly octopus* Octopus vulgaris *eyes us as a goatfish watches warily in the background.*

Nocturnal coral polyps Astrangia *bloom whenever the sun goes down.*

The tiny but deadly blue-ringed octopus prances daintily across a coral head.

In the darkness, a diver is framed by a gathering of soft corals and gorgonians.

It is hard to describe to those who do not dive the opulence of healthy coral reefs.

A friendly turtle enjoys a brief and gentle ride with Jessica Roessler. After our few moments together Jessica released the turtle and it circled us twice before swimming away.

A pair of bantayan butterflyfish are so perfectly aligned that they seem like one fish with two mouths. This fish is unique to the Philippines.

were literally incomparable places due to the diversity of their marine life. Teeming, color-filled shallows, plunging vertical walls, and gardens of lush, complex soft corals will always live in my memory.

Will the Philippines come back? When political and economic turmoil ends, divers will drift back and begin to survey the reefs. There are, and will be then, magical and wild places. I know somewhere a little deeper, a bit out of the way, are wondrous outpourings of life I would love to revisit. Recent dive groups have told me they are still sublime. The place where the three cuttlefish used to hang out every spring, that shadowed wall where thousands of soft corals throbbed in near-darkness, the rocks where rushing currents fed the multitudes—I know they are still there . . .

Meanwhile, divers will go to other politically and demographically stable places while these lovely islands endure their pain. If we are all lucky the time will soon come when we regularly enjoy the special wonders of the Philippine reefs and the friendly people. For now, the Philippines are visited mainly by the wise and the experienced who see beyond the evening news.

A pink nudibranch stands out even on a crowded reeftop. ▶

The South Pacific

Now we examine the great, throbbing heart of diving for at least the next decade. I have watched diving evolve over the past twenty years and I see an inexorable tide of divers moving to this vast arena. Its colossal distances combined with innumerable reefs and islands will thrill divers for many long years.

Early in their careers, divers experience Florida, the Bahamas, the Caribbean, even Hawaii. As they accumulate more experience they realize that the diving of the remote Pacific is far more colorful and exciting. Their first foray may be to Truk and Palau in Micronesia, for those islands have been well-publicized for more than twenty years.

Inevitably, however, the serious divers awaken to the lure of the South Pacific. Here, the best dive sites are the stuff of legend.

Today, the principle destinations are Fiji and Australia, but the Solomon Islands, Papua New Guinea, and Vanuatu

◄ *Among the strongest elements of Fijian reefs are current-swept pinnacles teeming with marine life.*

all have their avid enthusiasts, and immense potential for the future. Sophisticated divers are already seeking out these sublime places while they are still pristine and remote. Other divers even seek out the chilly waters of New Zealand, or little known islands such as Niue, the Cook Islands, New Caledonia, Indonesia, or Malaysia so as to be among the first to explore future Meccas.

In this book I will concentrate on the destinations divers can fully enjoy today, or soon. Some areas have practically no facilities for divers. Others have access only to nearby reefs which do not represent the best diving.

I have seen a number of these superb destinations develop through distinct stages. First, they are just a name, with perhaps fragmentary reports from intrepid explorers for whom comfort and facilities are relatively unimportant. This is, of course, the riskiest phase for divers. After all, the very first resort owner or boat skipper may be a dreamer whose skills will not deliver a dream diving adventure. Indeed some of the prominent "nightmare" scenarios often are told about places in this stage of development.

A second stage begins when two conditions are met: confirmation of rich, usually remote reefs, and the emergence of a quality live-aboard vessel or a well-managed small resort to accommodate divers. For me, this is often the best phase; limited facilities means limited traffic and unspoiled reefs. Right now, Papua New Guinea, the Solomons, and Vanuatu are all in this phase. Each has a dedicated, high quality live-aboard and one or more diving resorts on shore. The reefs are still being discovered, and returning divers tell stories of enchantment about these reefs.

Fiji

A destination matures when a variety of resorts and live-aboard vessels are in place to provide options for divers. Fiji is just now entering this level of development; it offers an interesting example which may be instructive to divers.

The tartan hawkfish Oxycirrhites *uses complex fans as shelter, blending neatly into their color scheme.*

Clear water along a Fijian reef. ▶

The entrance to Falange Atoll in the Lau Group of islands is a scenic gem.

When I first visited these islands in the early '70s there were but two dive services, both day boat oriented, and no active live-aboard. The reef selection was quite limited due to the nature of day boat diving. The places offered were very good but quite close to the respective shore bases.

Over the years a small (six person) live-aboard emerged with wonderful service, and several resorts installed dive equipment and programs.

Today, three live-aboards offer varying itineraries and it seems that every outer island or beach resort has declared itself a dive center.

There are problems here for the unwary. Not every island has excellent reefs, yet advertising tends to obscure rather than define the differences between products. There are

The dramatic plumes of a soft coral colony contrast with the midnight blue of the sea.

(Previous left) *This spectacular damselfish* Centropyge bicolor *is normally very shy and takes intense stalking to capture on film.*

(Previous right) *Great schools of fish flutter among dense stands of soft coral.*

some sensational dive sites in Fiji, of which most are quite remote. I have taken cruises, which included the best sites of Beqa, Astrolabe Reef, Moturiki, Wakaya, Gau, and the southern Lau Islands; what impressed me most was the variety of marine life, topography, and color on these dives.

Beqa is the most accessible of these sites, and the most variable. Beqa is an undersea plateau several miles across, upon which two islands break the surface. Scattered across the remaining plateau area are clusters of coral pinnacles ranging from thirty to seventy feet high. The crests of these pinnacles reach nearly to the water's surface. The pinnacle structures remind me of others we will encounter in Australia's Coral Sea, with one crucial difference—currents.

The plateau of Beqa is swept by tidal currents of a knot or more. During slack tides, when the currents do not flow, the pinnacles can seem almost barren.

But when the tide turns and begins to flow, an astonishing awakening occurs. Colonies of soft coral which were dull-looking lumps begin to waken. Inflating their intricately-branched bodies with water they spread their arms across the flow. Colony after colony, in pink or lavender or yellow or blood red, reveals thousands of complex polyps.

Soon the pinnacles are carpeted in color, radiant in the most spectacular tapestry in the undersea world. In the moving waters now dance multitudes of small fish, feeding

A pair of pufferfish Canthigaster *pause for a moment in their busy day.*

The Raffles' butterflyfish Chaetodon rafflesi *is a trademark species of Fiji's reefs.*

Darting about in the embrace of an anemone's tentacles is the tomato clownfish Amphiprion frenatus.

A flame goby Nemateleotris magnifica *hovers above its burrow at the bottom of a cave.*

The colors and textures of Fiji's reefs are lush and vivid.

A spine-cheek Scolopsis bilineatus *is cleaned of parasites by an attentive cleaner wrasse* Labroides.

on the plankton carried by the moving waters. For divers, the pinnacles such as Caesar's Rocks are a challenge; to take photographs is like trying to mountain-climb during a cyclonic wind. Every movement is an intense exertion.

Of course, the photographic results are ample reward. Dazzling colors fill the frame, and the eye struggles to pick out individual creatures amid thousands.

You will hear, as I have, from divers who have been to Beqa when the currents were not flowing; and they were disappointed. You need only speak with one who has dived the reef in full bloom to realize that diving there is simply a matter of weather and tides. Hit it right and you will make dive after dive to maximize your experience with these riches.

Some miles to the northeast from Beqa is another series of reefs near Moturiki island. On my first dive here, I jumped into the water near some small pinnacle structures similar to those of Beqa. My first impression was that there

wasn't much here. Then I began to look more closely with awakening respect.

Some pinnacle sections stood up to the currents and were rewarded with carpets of rainbow-hued soft corals. Other areas were in the lee of the structures; here in the still water I would find lionfish in flaring finery, Moorish idols, angelfish, butterflyfish, and other colorful citizens. Then, on the open bottom around the pinnacles were mantis shrimp lairs, unusual eels, nudibranchs, flatworms; what had seemed at first glance a modest reef became a treasure house.

Fiji has many such wonders scattered amid its far-flung islands. The reefs I have described thus far are those

An extraordinary proboscis enables the long-snout butterfly-fish Forcipiger longirostris *to pluck coral polyps without having its eyes stung.* ▶

flooded with color. There are others whose character is very different. Places such as Wakaya, Gau, and the Lau islands have reefs which are soaring stony battlements above the blue abyss. Here and there are pockets of color where currents nurture soft coral colonies. However, most of these reefs are dominated by stony corals whose colors are more muted.

In return for less (or at least less obvious) color, these deep-water parapets reward us with action. One reef wall at Wakaya has a second, projecting reef structure at right angles some 75 feet below the main crest. Each time I have dived here, mild currents flowed along the main reef. When the currents encounter the deep formation, it is a massive obstacle to smooth flow and the currents are intensified. One consequence is a huge school of barracuda which hover above the formation. Parenthetically, identical formations in Palau, the Sudan, and Papua New Guinea have precisely the same lure for barracuda.

Other reef sites offer completely different experiences. At one island in the Laus, a massive chasm slices through the

◀ *If you look closely at a crowded reeftop you may find a scorpionfish* Scorpaena *camouflaged to capture passing fish.*

A school of unicorn fish on a reef slope.

Different reefs have different aspects, some crowded and tumultuous, others placid and orderly.

reef, creating a colossal stony arch some 130 feet beneath the surface. Near this formation is a cluster of huge anemones with brilliantly colored tomato clownfish, *Amphiprion frenatus*. It is an interesting commentary on divers that often one coral formation or one fish can lock a site into our memory for life.

Astrolabe Reef is another fascinating part of southern Fiji's array of superb dive locations. Local chiefs have restricted access to Astrolabe for a few years, and I must say that most of its sites were not missed as other areas of Fiji were explored. Still, the Color Wall on the southern face of north Astrolabe Reef is an experience worth several hours of

65

Colorful fairy basslets Anthias *flutter above Fiji's reefs. Their fluttering, rapid movements make portraiture a challenge.*

◀ *A hawkfish watches for prey at the base of a purple gorgonian.*

currents. The abundant food supply carried by the currents has led to an explosion of life on this reef.

Currents are a powerful force in Fiji diving, defining in most cases the country's most vivid dive sites. As we survey the Pacific's greatest diving we will find other magnificent reefs whose entire character is due to the currents flowing over them.

For those of you who might contemplate Fiji for one of your earliest Pacific adventures, you may find you can best sample the diving in the southern islands via live-aboard dive cruiser, while the northern islands have a variety of shore resorts with reasonable access to such star attractions as Rainbow Reef.

open ocean cruising to reach. As its name suggests, the wall is quite vertical, and blazes with bright colors from soft corals and encrusting sponges.

Similarly, the eastern line of Astrolabe's main reef has a rare segment where a particular purple soft coral has proliferated to cover nearly the entire reef face.

What I have tried to suggest with these specifics is the vast mosaic that diving the southern Fijis can yield. The northern islands, of which Taveuni is the best known, have some rather different attractions. Rainbow Reef, also well-known, is another vertical reef line often swept with stiff

A clownfish Amphiprion bicinctus *carefully guards its precious eggs.*

Australia's remote coral reefs offer some of the most consistently clear water in the world.

Australia

I have approached the Pacific's greatest diving with a sequence clearly in mind. First, I describe today's star destinations, places long known for superb marine life—Palau, Truk Lagoon, Fiji, Australia—which also are places divers go first when they emerge from the Caribbean.

Truk, Palau, and Fiji are, in some senses, easy. Why? Because you should get some excellent diving regardless of which dive service you select. Australia, on the other hand, is the most difficult and tricky of all Pacific destinations. More divers have returned from Australia baffled and disappointed than from any other destination in the world. Why?

The Great Barrier Reef

In simplest terms, the problem is the Great Barrier Reef. This 1,200-mile complex of reefs and islands is truly the world's largest; somehow in the minds of divers some errant alchemy has transmuted *size* into *quality*. I have talked with

literally hundreds of otherwise well informed divers who have become convinced that the Great Barrier Reef is the World's Greatest Diving.

It falls to me to break the news that in nearly twenty years I have found only three top dive sites on the Barrier Reef, while I have endured many that were quite modest. There are parts of the Barrier Reef I have not dived (in the far north) but in the areas from Rockhampton all the way north to Lizard Island the pattern has been the same.

So, let's set the record straight. There are indeed three world-class dives on the Great Barrier Reef; dives that are worth flying to the Pacific to experience:

1. The wreck of the *Yongala*, south of Townsville: This miracle of life takes place because the 240-foot-long wreck lies on an otherwise empty undersea plain some

A diver swims through a narrow tunnel lined with soft corals and gorgonians.

This sailfin leaf-fish Taenionotus *yawns luxuriantly despite the nearby camera.*

The blue-headed wrasse Thalassa *darts swiftly about the reef hunting for food.*

ninety feet below the surface. The plain extends for miles in all directions. The wreck has achieved the analogue of the African watering hole where various species commingle in marvelous truce. Divers encounter nearly tame eagle rays, sting rays, groupers, sea snakes, schools of grunts, snappers, cobia, spade-fish, and jacks. You may come face to face with up to nine giant Queensland grouper (Jewfish), guitar sharks, turtles, and other exotic creatures.

2. The Cod Hole north of Cairns: Here, man has created a wonder quite analogous to Sting Ray City in the Cayman Islands. The well fed performers are nearly twenty huge potato cod (*Epinephelus tukula*), three massive Napoleon wrasse (*Cheilinus undulatus*), and at least three sassy green moray eels (*Gymnothorax funebris*). Add to those superstars a supporting cast of several hundred smaller fish fighting for the scraps the larger fish miss, and you have one of the sea's most active dive sites.

3. Pixie Pinnacle: An hour south of the Cod Hole is a pinnacle formation in a passage between the Ribbon Reefs. Probably because of sustained currents through the pass, Pixie has accumulated an amazing array of marine life for a single ninety-foot formation around which you can swim in a minute or two.

On a recent day at Pixie I found three inseparable pairs of football-sized deadly stonefish *Synanceia verrucosa*, a curious mantis shrimp *Squilla* that I followed all around the pinnacle, a white sailfin leaf fish *Taenionotus*, three pairs of scarlet clownfish *Premnas*, and a cornucopia of other species.

Now, you may be wondering why I consider the Great Barrier Reef poor if these three sites are so wonderful. It is because each of these will fill half a day, or even a full day, and then where do you go?

All right, you say, if that is true why is Australia so famous for great diving?

Quite simply, it is because of the magnificent oceanic atolls eighty to two hundred miles out to sea *beyond* the Great Barrier Reef.

The Coral Sea

It is to these far off paradises that I have made some twenty-eight pilgrimages in the past two decades. There are no islands to speak of in the trackless expanses of the open Coral Sea; only a sandbar here and there. The hundreds of miles of atoll reefs rise from abyssal depths to within a few feet of the surface — and stop. Their gleaming ramparts are laved with open ocean water of crystal clarity. From the end-

◀ The mantis shrimp Squilla *is a ferocious predator with the fastest strike of all marine creatures when it attacks prey.*

A rare encounter with a twelve-foot tiger shark Galeocerdo cuvieri *will be the highlight of any day.*

less blue sea come large pelagics to intermingle with local reef species. You may be photographing a small fish and suddenly see a whale shark, or slip quietly down a steep wall to discover a manta ray passing by.

I personally have enjoyed sensational diving in the Coral Sea, yet have known some divers to return disappointed; therefore let me characterize the diving I rate so highly with accuracy. First, the water clarity at all of the Coral Sea reefs I will describe is generally excellent. Second, the incidence of large pelagic species on shallow reefs is higher than almost any place I have seen in the world. Third, if you see a fish or a soft coral or a gorgonian fan it may be the biggest you

A deadly stonefish Synanceia verrucosa *is so well camouflaged it is hard to see on a cluttered reef.*

71

Massive groupers Epinephelus tukula *swim with us at the famous Cod Hole dive site.*

The butterflyfish Chaetodon speculum *can be found browsing on polyps of black coral.*

Gray sharks Carcharrhinus amblyrhynchos *can become very aggressive during a feeding.*

A cleaner wrasse Labroides *picks parasites from the open mouth of a moray eel.* ▶

A large harlequin wrasse Bodianus vulpinus *sweeps in and eyes me as it passes.*

have ever seen of its species. Given those three superior qualities, how could anyone not be delighted?

In a word, the answer is *density*. Where Fiji may offer you thousands of soft corals in a brilliant tapestry, the Coral Sea may at any site offer you one monster colony of soft coral six to eight feet in height—and at a depth of 140 feet!

As I think back over diving in the Coral Sea, certain dives emerge from thousands as the examples one uses to illustrate greatness . . .

North Horn at Osprey Reef

There are places on the planet that stand out in any recitation of the world's best: the Blue Point in Palau, Zabargad in the Red Sea, Banaua Bommie in Papua New Guinea, and others. Each of these special sites has certain topography or marine life that elevates it above others; those which are known for sharks have an added cachet when divers get together to trade stories.

North Horn is the northernmost extremity of Osprey Reef, some 80 miles northeast of Lizard Island. At North Horn, currents flowing northward around both sides of the atoll formation meet. This confluence of currents seems to produce a gathering-place for all manner of pelagic species. Its topography is abrupt and powerful; plunging from the surface, the coral mass develops into a stepped dropoff into deep water. There is a pulpit or ledge at 70–90 feet that is a natural feeding point for sharks. At all times, up to twenty sharks patrol there—grays, silvertips, and reef white-tips, plus several huge groupers, some rapacious moray eels, and an occasional school of barracuda. Occasionally, tuna, manta rays, and even whale sharks have been known to pass by. All in all, North Horn is a place where the patient observer is rewarded with pelagic species in abundance.

74

The anemone-fish Premnas biaculeatus *hides its resplendent colors amid the arms of its host anemone.*

Sometimes a clownfish Amphiprion bicinctus *will bark its anger at intruders.*

This pair of butterflyfish Hemitaurichthys *feeds on coral polyps.*

A pair of bannerfish Heniochus *hover in a dark cavern.*

Action Point at Marion Reef

Action Point at Marion Reef is the analogous northern extremity at this wondrous atoll 320 miles off the coast. Marion is eastward and somewhat south of Townsville, but it takes a lot of cruising to reach. For nearly twenty years, however, it has paid dividends to those who persisted. Where the windward reef line terminates at the northern tip of Marion, another group of sharks, principally grays, has been resident since at least 1972. I would be hard-pressed to guess how many shark-feedings I have enjoyed here. Indeed, all of the shark feedings I experienced in the early 70s were at Action Point. It was here that mythic monsters became real animals, admiration replaced anxiety, and a long love affair with sharks germinated.

The Bommies at Marion Reef

Within the clear water lagoon at Marion, some fifty or more reef complexes soar from depths of 180–200 feet to nearly reach the surface. Some are single spires, some double, and some have ten or more spires with sandy valleys between them. While their marine life is not as profuse as that of some reefs in the Philippines, the Red Sea, Fiji, or Papua New Guinea, anything you see here tends to be large. The angelfish, the Moorish idols, the colonies of yellow *Turbinaria* coral, the massive soft corals tend to be the biggest of their type I have seen. Add to that the fact that we photograph in extremely clear water, and the Coral Sea's long preeminence is understandable.

The bad news, of course, is that the distances in the Coral Sea are also large. A Coral Sea dive program involves six nights or more of all-night cruising between major reefs.

75

A large nudibranch Notodoris *browses on algae.*

Some people dread these crossings, but I think of them as the major reason that diving in the Coral Sea has not declined over the past two decades. A brief season (the fall) and long hours of cruising limit the population of divers to the most avid, that is, precisely those who appreciate this magnificent diving.

A final secret for those who would dive these longtime favorites of mine: the more you swim, the more you see. I mentioned that the sublime creatures here were less prolific

◄ *A massive crown of thorns starfish* Acanthaster planci.

than on reefs elsewhere. Therefore, unlike those other locales, you cannot pick a ten-meter square of reef and find lots to photograph.

The Coral Sea rewards the wanderer, the diver who swims around the pinnacles, into the canyons, down the walls. These are the divers who find the zebra sharks, the yellow nudibranchs, the lush anemone/clownfish symbionts. These are the divers who return full of praise for these oceanic reefs of the Coral Sea.

Selfishly, I hope that reefs like these never become convenient, are never invaded by thousands of human visitors, that they will always be out there safely beyond the horizon . . .

77

An arm's-length away the shark studies its intended prey.

◀ *With incredibly intense focus, the shark closes in on its target.*

The famed shark victim Rodney Fox comes face to face with his old nemesis.

The Great White Shark

Before leaving Australia there is one special adventure utterly unlike all others. Its drama is played out far to the south, in waters whose "other side" is Antarctica.

Since 1976, I have made an annual pilgrimage to the shrine of that final lord of the sea, the great white shark, *Carcharrhinus carcharias*. This kind of diving utilizes shark cages, for the sharks are 13 to 16 feet in length; often we will have two or more at a time. On a recent trip we had seven feeding simultaneously!

I have never met any animal in the sea as impressive as the great whites. They are cautious and yet implacable. They are capable of feats of stupefying strength, such as leaping clear of the water. Every time you think you have seen it all, a great white will put on a more awesome display than you have ever witnessed before.

White sharks can feed—eagerly—in any position.

The irresistible force . . .

In case the thought comes up, of course my expeditions are safe. The boat, the cages, and the techniques are designed to film these sublimely powerful creatures, not make sacrifices to them. In fact, white sharks get to be big by being very cautious. An interesting sidelight to our shark cage adventures is this: the reason we get this size shark to work with us is that they are like impulsive teenagers. We never even get a hint of the great 23-footers who glide by, ignoring our pathetic bait in search of more significant prey.

The great white sharks prey on pinnipeds (sea lions, sea elephants), whales, rays, porpoises, and anything in trouble. They are supremely efficient, perfectly designed, and the embodiment of the marine predator.

However, the real reason for the sharks' effect on us is — us. Perhaps it is an atavistic memory, the first terror in the first prehuman echoing like a muffled scream down a corridor of centuries. Perhaps somehow we create the terror in seeing predation thus perfected, I do not know. I do know that the excitement of being twelve inches away from the teeth of such a shark is on a totally different plane from tiger-thrill or ape-thrill. We are in a different world for these moments, and this is the commanding alien presence of that world.

We can try to wish it away, but the terror always rises in us; and it is just that dark shadow of ancient dread which spices those hours in the cage. I have spent some 360 hours in cages filming white sharks; it is a parade of moments I would not trade for any others in the sea.

The real world of this great predator is the gloomy kingdom below the surface. Just try to swim to that boat . . .

In a rare "double," two sharks present themselves simultaneously.

In the darkness, at home in bed, the images will sometimes return unbidden; that awesome torpedo with eyes soars across the imagination. The surprise is that the replayed image is one of beauty and grace, with only that piquant touch of menace. All in all a pleasurable memory, and one never forgotten no matter what other wonderful marine citizens one meets. If there is one ultimate, then, among all these luminous adventures in the sea, you will find it here.

The Solomon Islands

My first impression flying westward from Honiara on Guadalcanal was: *look at all those islands!* This is a hallmark of the South Pacific: the Philippines boast of their seven thousand islands, Indonesia has thirteen thousand, and I haven't any idea how many form New Guinea, but the Solomons would be difficult even to count. Hundreds of tiny islands dot the placid ocean's surface, making larger islands seem like hens surrounded by a myriad of chicks.

An immediate consequence of this proliferation is that no one knows how many dive sites may in fact be found here. There may be quite literally hundreds to be found in future years. What a treasure to look forward to and savor!

This is a suitable moment to pause and put expert opinion in context. Only those who live in a place such as the Solomons have even a chance to know its reefs. The rest of us, even professional travelers like myself, see a mere sampling chosen by those local divers. The sample will only consist of two or three sites per day, and even those may be constrained by distance, the speed of available boats, and other factors.

When I lived in Curacao and Bonaire in the Caribbean (1969–72) I dove every day; only at the very end of those three years did I feel I really *knew* the dive sites of a mere two islands . . .

Off the coast of a tiny island, a native fishing boat's occupants eye the strangers.

81

In defense of travelling experts, I quickly point out that the local divers always take us to their best available sites in hope that we will bring them customers. Only because we have seen their chosen best does someone like me feel qualified to venture comparisons between these complex and variegated countries.

There is in the Solomons an infinite range of sites which can be gathered under perhaps three general headings: wrecks, passes, and island walls.

Many of the wrecks here have been devastated by salvage operations, by earthquakes, and by normal oxidation. Unlike Truk Lagoon, one would not travel all the way to the Solomons to dive the shallow wrecks (though some are impressive); instead, the real attraction of these islands is a colorful tapestry of marine life in extraordinary settings.

As we have seen all over the Pacific, some wonderful diving is found in the passes through which tidal water flows into and out of lagoons. At Marovo Lagoon, some of these passes are up to a half-mile wide and perhaps 250 feet in depth. Immense volumes of water flow through the passes but at modest velocity. That provides rich feeding for fish and invertebrates which line the walls, yet easy diving conditions for human visitors.

The exceptions to this are the narrow passes one hundred yards wide or less. Here the tidal flow really moves; I vividly remember hovering outside the corner of the Uepi Pass, then feeling myself accelerate as I reached the corner of the entrance. Within seconds I was moving at a rate of at least 3–4 knots, and anything I grasped would have been torn off the wall. That kind of intense foodstream creates astonishingly prolific segments of reef at the corners; fans, crinoids, soft corals, and countless millions of plankton-eating fish

The lagoon at Mbula Island is one of the most peaceful, lovely places in the Pacific.

Jessica Roessler and a confident lionfish Pterois volitans *come face to face on a complex reef wall.*

◀ *A gorgonian fan is the perfect backdrop for a flight of fairy basslets.*

83

fluttering madly in the swift waters assault the mind with countless colorful images.

It is interesting to note that the vertical outer dropoffs between these passes are often relatively barren. There seem to be miles of vertical stone precipice, on which only rare examples of the colorful creatures who throng the passes are seen.

The remembrance of those sepulchral walls remind me that in all of the world's famous dive locales there is both good and bad diving. A vacation in Australia or Fiji or New Guinea can be a triumph or tragedy depending upon precisely where you jump into the water. My standout memories of diving's great classics are of selected reefs, none larger than a football field and many far smaller. Each of these great classics may be surrounded by miles of open ocean or miles of mediocre reefs. The archetypal example of this is the *Yongala* wreck in Australia, surrounded for ten miles in every direction by empty sand bottom.

Two Solomons dives instantly separate themselves from all other recollection, The Corner at Mbula Island, and Mberi Island. Mberi Island boasts a school of perhaps five hundred barracuda who have remained in place for at least the past year. The Corner is just that: water flowing along a vertical wall hits a projecting face, is forced to flow to the west for perhaps fifty yards, then turns The Corner and proceeds. The projecting face and corner are a veritable Christmas tree of giant fans and soft coral colonies from near the surface to beyond 200 foot depths. It is a moving, brilliantly-hued dive.

As a bonus, and to provide balm for the soul of weary divers, there is near The Corner a special grotto. This small area interrupts the prevailing precipice with a sandy, shallow ledge that turns sunlight to aquamarine. Small, scattered

◀ *A motionless* Tridacna *clam is decorated with convoluted patterns of rich color.*

coral heads entice snorkelers; the result is an ineradicable memory of a moment in paradise. Whenever I think of the Solomons, The Corner and its grotto leap to mind as symbols of this island-dotted land. How many more of these precious places are there, quietly awaiting future exploration?

Vanuatu

The Republic of Vanuatu was until 1980 known as the New Hebrides. It was in pre-independence days famous for a joint (known as Condominium) government of the French and British. There were separate French and British customs, police, and other services. The joke was that if you ever got in trouble, let the French arrest you—their jail food was so much better. I never tried it.

Soft corals Dendronephthya *carpet a vertical coral wall.*

Red hydrocorals grow on the metal of a sunken wreck.

A yellow nudibranch against the backdrop of a red gorgonian fan.

A ribbon of eggs deposited by a Spanish dancer nudibranch Hexabranchus sanguineus.▶

Among divers, the mention of Vanuatu elicits one of two answers: a dumbfounded, "Where?" or the words "*S.S. President Coolidge.*" For twenty years I have sent people to Vanuatu for as little as two days so they could see this behemoth among wrecks.

Unlike the wrecks of Truk Lagoon or the Red Sea or New Guinea or the Solomons, carpeted with color and life, the *Coolidge* is somber, its raiment only of the crypt. It is covered with fine green-brown sediment, punctuated here and there with a colorful nudibranch or browsing tropical fish.

The only coral growing on the *Coolidge* is in the deep shadows under its bridge and bow. Forests of the deep-green-colored *Dendrophyllia* coral merely add density to the monstrous shadows. There is, on the *Coolidge*, an eerie, spooky quality I have experienced very few times in the tropical world.

The funereal presence of this wreck comes not from human fatalities (only three died out of five thousand); no, it is as if the ship still mourned for its own lost glory as Cunard Lines' premiere passenger ship. Melancholy and the

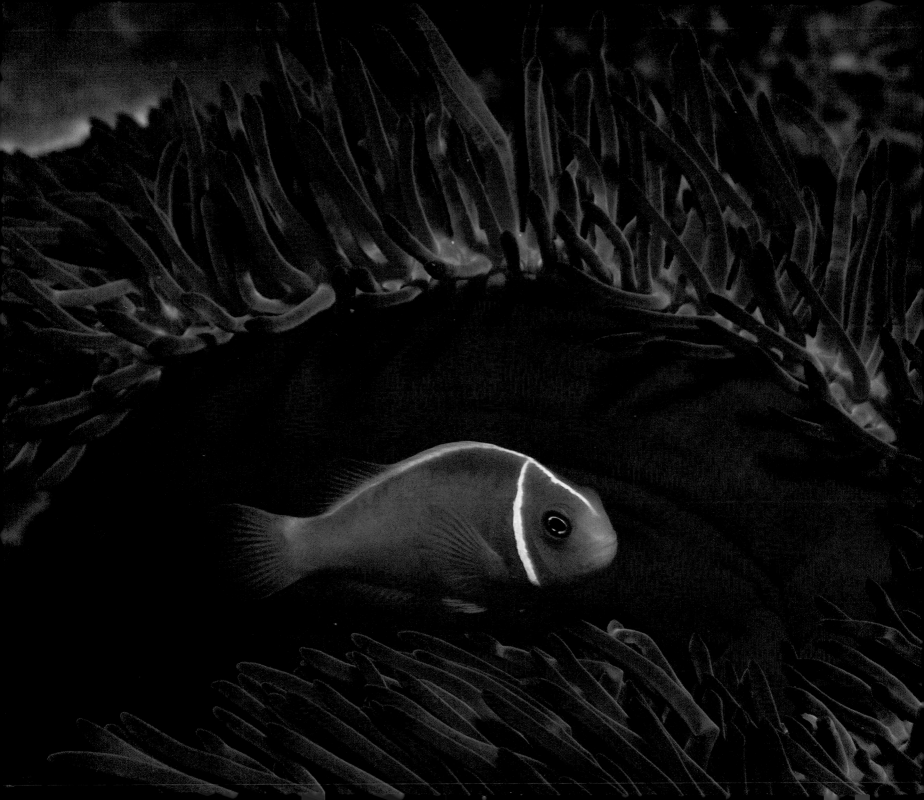

hint of doom are always there when we dive this grandest of all diveable wrecks.

Just down the coast from the *Coolidge* site is Million-Dollar Point. At the end of the Second World War, America had a vast facility at Espiritu Santo. As the troops headed home, huge numbers of trucks, jeeps, bulldozers, and other material became superfluous. The Americans asked the British and French to bid on the surplus, but those worthies cleverly concluded they need bid nothing—the Americans would leave it in any event.

The American commander, bless his heart, ran it all into the ocean in a massive avalanche of steel. To this day scattered fish and coral frequent the site. There is, however, a persistent sense of unreality, as if all this, after all, simply can't be here . . .

While the *Coolidge* and Million-Dollar Point are the mnemonics for divers to remember Vanuatu, there is far more here. Physically, the islands continue southward the chain of Papua New Guinea and the Solomons; one would expect sheer walls, some passes, coral gardens, big creatures, and indeed they are here. Vanuatu will join Australia, Fiji, Palau, and Truk as a famous name in Pacific diving.

The reason is *variety*. On a recent cruise amid the widely scattered islands, I encountered a 700-pound jewfish, several families of cuttlefish, a tame octopus, a sunken World War II Hellcat bomber, valleys filled with profuse and multicolored hydrocorals, turtles, nudibranchs and their eggs, several species of clownfish, massive schools of buffalo parrotfish, gardens of branching *Acropoia* corals, massive dropoffs— and an unmistakable feeling that I had only scratched the surface.

A Hellcat bomber rests in shallow water off the coast of Pentecost Island.

A squadron of lionfish rest on the forward gun mount of the S. S. President Coolidge.

◀*This clownfish sweeps gracefully up a valley formed by the mantle of its host anemone.*

"Dudley" the dugong extends a warm welcome to a visiting diver.

Every morning we anchored at a new island, wandering in a 700-mile odyssey through an undiscovered paradise.

While at this moment less known than neighboring island nations such as Papua New Guinea, Fiji, and the Solomons, Vanuatu will emerge to its own stardom. Those who spend the time to go on the complete circuit through the islands will be well rewarded; photographers in search of new images may be, as I was, pleasantly surprised at the range of subjects.

Papua New Guinea

Of all the new destinations to emerge in recent years, this may be the best. Papua New Guinea lies north of Queensland, Australia and west of the Solomons.

From the diver's point of view this astonishing country is two separate entities: the massive main island with soaring peaks, torrential rivers, and an interior no-man's-land, and also a separate garden of scattered islands like the Solomons.

While the mainland is famous for carvings, culture, and literally half of the languages spoken on earth, the scattered islands are a magnet for serious divers.

The blue nose is a startling characteristic of the reclusive angelfish Apolemichthys trimaculatus.

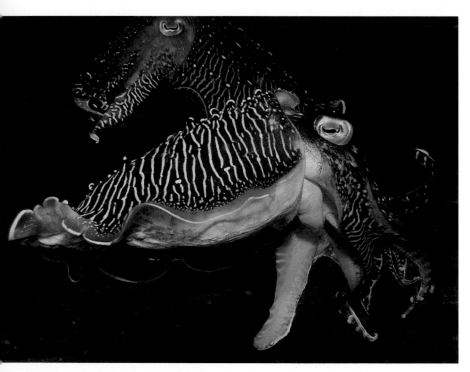

A pair of cuttlefish flare for the human visitor.

90

Night dives yield sightings of nocturnal creatures such as this graceful crinoid Comanthina.

A huge pufferfish Arothron stellatus *is cleaned by two cleaner wrasse* Labroides dimidiatus.

At noon with the tropic sun above, shallow reefs can become mesmerizingly beautiful.

One of the most stunningly decorated sea cucumbers I have ever seen browses on corraline sand.

The reason for the powerful attraction is the marine life, known both for its lushness and its many unusual species. Taking my own trips to New Guinea compared with twenty years of the rest of the world, I discover:

- It is the *only* place I have found and photographed chambered nautilus, swell shark, the majid crab, the porcelain crab, the pinto clownfish, and the bizarre scorpionfish, *Rhinopias aphanes.*
- It also yields a tiny goby *(Gobisoma)* which lives on red gorgonians, the ghost pipefish, *Solenostomus,* dozens of seeing-eye goby/blind prawn pairs, a nearly tame cuttlefish, octopus, huge pink lacy hydrocorals, and the otherworldly horned sea cucumber.

The skunk clownfish Amphiprion sandaricinos *is one of the gaudiest of reef fish.*

Found at depths of 1,000 feet or more, the chambered nautilus is an ancient species of cephalopod.

That is the kind of place that stands out among all others in a photographer's mind. It is certainly one of the three or four greatest dive destinations in the world. Having said that, it is imperative that I echo my earlier warning: I have seen a lot of *dreadful* diving in Papua New Guinea, and many divers are taken to the dreadful places because they are convenient to various hotels and population centers.

The places where I saw all of the species listed above were invariably several hours from shore, remote, pristine, untouched. I suspect their inaccessibility was a key ingredient in their richness. Would I climb on a plane and fly to New Guinea to dive those sites? You bet. Would I do it to dive other more convenient sites? No. The bad places are as bad as the good are good . . .

Before leaving the rare, even bizarre species that are the hallmark of Papua New Guinea diving, there are two that so excite divers that they deserve special attention.

This gaudy wrasse is known as Axel's pigfish Bodianus axelli.▶

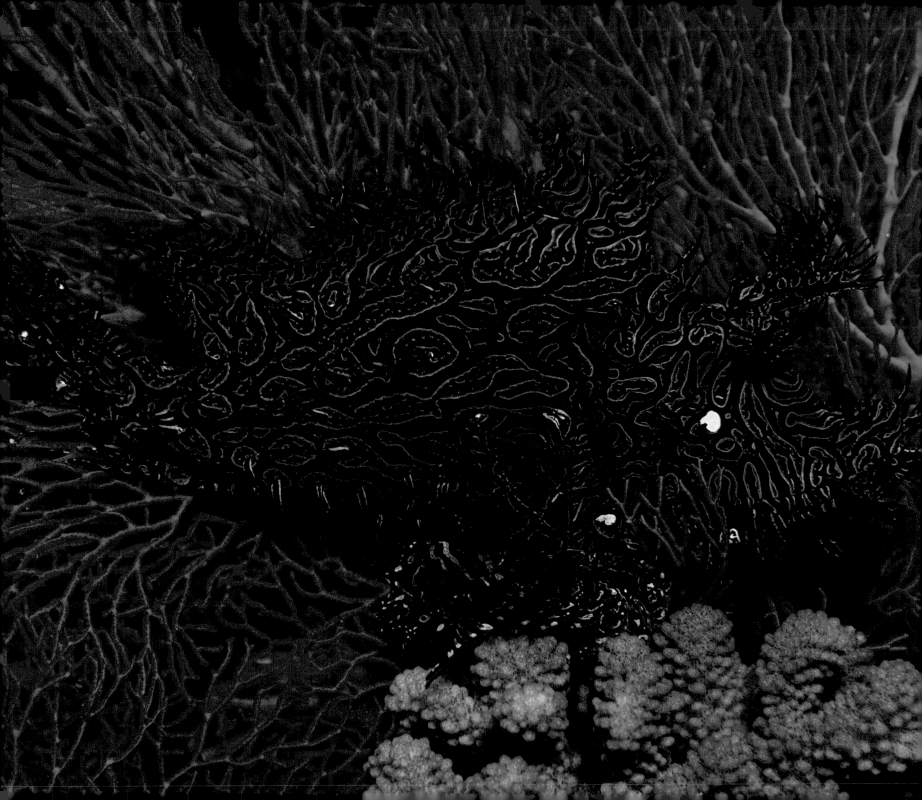

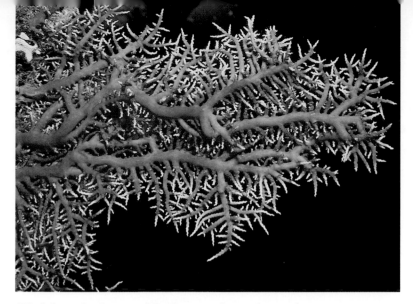

Pink lace hydrocoral Stylaster *abounds on the current-swept walls of Papua New Guinea's reefs.*

The goby Byraninops *hides by blending into the slender stalks of a gorgonian.*

The first is the Merlot's Scorpionfish, *Rhinopias aphanes*. This gorgeously ugly creature was first pointed out to me by Bob Halstead off Port Moresby several years ago. When Bob showed it to me it was only the third specimen ever found.

Recently I joined Bob and his wife Dinah for a dive cruise through the many islands of Milne Bay. On the first day he told me he had a site with another *Rhinopias*; we both prayed for good weather, because the site was totally exposed.

Our luck held, the weather was sheer perfection. Bob and I jumped into the water and began our search. The way to find *Rhinopias* is to reverse its own stratagem: from a distance this complex fish looks like a common green crinoid *Comanthina*, therefore examine each and every crinoid to see which one is the fish.

◀ *The royalty of exotic fish species, Merlot's scorpionfish* Rhinopias aphanes *looks like a harmless crinoid when motionless on the reef. Small fish swim past, and it gulps them down.*

The nearly invisible majid crab has evolved to mimic the soft coral polyps upon which it feeds.

95

That may sound silly, for every reef is adorned with hundreds of crinoids. We searched and searched and could not find *Rhinopias*, so we slunk back to the boat.

As we wearily peeled off our gear, dejected and defeated, one of the crew said brightly, "Oh, didn't you see the fish? Mary Jane saw the fish."

Like lightning, Bob and I grabbed fresh tanks and leaped into the water. Sure enough, a column of bubbles announced that one of our avid clients had indeed found *Rhinopias*. Those of you who are divers and underwater photographers have already discerned the emotions that ran riot in that hour; those of you who aren't, please look at the picture and imagine.

The other Milne Bay dive I must mention is the plunge to the Blackjack Bomber. Off a small fishing village at Cape Vogel the shallow reef slopes quite sharply to a flat, sandy bottom at 154 feet. There, in sublime glory, is an intact, upright B-17 bomber. Lost in a storm, out of fuel, its crew pancaked the bomber, walked out on its right wing, jumped

The sunken B-17 known as the Blackjack Bomber has a long and colorful history. Its crew crash-landed and walked to safety.

The nudibranch Chromodoris *glides slowly across an encrusting sponge.*

The benediction of a morning rain shower brings us a gentle rainbow.

to safety on the shallow reef, and walked ashore. The bomber sank, fluttering like some gigantic leaf to this undersea sanctuary.

Today, we anchor just forward of her, dive down a weighted line, and (if the water is clear) enjoy one of the thrills of a lifetime.

All of these wonders personify today's Papua New Guinea diving; we can only imagine the creatures still to be discovered amid her thousands of remote islands.

The Maldives

While the Pacific is exploding with new destinations (Indonesia, Malaysia, Western Australia) that will be in tomorrow's books, there is one great classic that should be our Indian Ocean entry.

Many years ago when I was a boy, the intrepid Austrian adventurer Hans Hass sailed his yacht, *Xarifa*, to the Maldive Islands. With Hass was the biologist Irenaus Eibl-Eibesfeldt, whose subsequent book, *Land of a Thousand Atolls*, was a touchstone of my youth.

Actually, there are 1,196 atolls in this ocean kingdom. There are so many that boats cannot travel safely by night; most of the atoll rings are just beneath the surface, and constitute an immense hazard.

In the bright sunlight, however, miles and miles of aquamarine reef line seem to stretch forever before us. The shallow reefs are inhabited by fish that seem the most docile and cooperative in the world. The careful diver is rewarded by a parade of exotic species whose browsing is oblivious to us. *Your intrusion is but a moment*, they seem to say, *We shall be here long after you have returned to your world . . .*

It is important to mention that most of the prime diving in the Maldives is quite shallow. The corals and the fish that feed upon them seem to diminish rapidly below forty feet.

In the atoll lagoons, the shallow sandy bottom can extend for miles.

Anemones with clownfish and black damselfish carpet many Maldivean reefs.

There are sharks, mantas, sometimes even whale sharks associated with the tidal passes in a pattern we have seen worldwide. Nature's marine cornucopia seems inextricably linked with moving water. From Cocos Island to the Maldives, from Yap to the Sudan, tidal waters feed the multitudes.

Among 1,196 atolls, the number of passes, walls, and shallow gardens are beyond enumeration. One could literally explore here for years. Until now, most resort development, indeed most diving, has been concentrated in the central atolls near the capital, Male. Future exploration to the southern tip of the archipelago, where the former British military base on Gan looks across open empty sea should yield more marvels.

If Yap is for manta rays, south Australia for white sharks, and the Philippines for crinoids, the Maldives is the place for fish. Beneath an ocean like glass is a serene miracle. a place where fish and humans interact without fear.

The Maldives have been a tourist destination for Europeans and Japanese for some years. There are many resorts of all sizes built on small islets around Male and nearby atolls.

That means the dive sites within easy reach of these hotels have seen a lot of diving activity. The serious diver would be well advised to use live-aboard dive boats to reach reefs that are undamaged.

Those who take the initiative and reach such reefs will find them very different from those of the South Pacific. Corals form sloping gardens and undercut shelves; the sun-dappled gardens are rich in butterflyfish, triggerfish, angelfish, and other tropical species. Many of these species

◀ *The angelfish* Euxiphipops xanthometopon *swims fearlessly past.*

A diver explores the shadowed world under a ledge where *shy soldierfish* Myripristis *hide from the sun.*

we do not find in the Pacific. The shadowed ledges shelter another range of reclusive citizens such as shy soldierfish and squirrelfish who shun the brilliant sunlight.

Adventurous divers will find a range of diving and facilities here. With careful research you will reach reefs that justify a pilgrimage halfway around the planet.

Thailand

Another destination in the Indian Ocean lies off the western coast of Thailand, an overnight cruise north of Phuket. The Similan Islands are a small chain of islands whose diving consists of two quite different types.

On the eastern side of each island are shallow coral gardens leading to sloping dropoffs. These reefs and slopes are rich in both branching and dome corals, and the waters above the reef are quite rich in small tropical fish.

On the western side of each island the dives are totally different. These western reefs are dominated by massive boulders swept by swift currents. The fish here dart from shelter to shelter to avoid being swept away. On the surface of the boulders, small soft coral colonies flutter pennantlike in the roaring waters. Indian Ocean species we have seen in the Maldives are plentiful, from the spectacularly-designed *Euxiphipops xanthometopon* to the boldly striped butterflyfish, *Chaetodon meyeri*. Because of the swift currents, fish photography is far more of a challenge amid the western boulders than on the eastern coral gardens, and in neither place do the fish behave like their nearly tame cousins in the Maldives.

In muted colors but bold design, the striped angelfish Pomacanthodes annularis *cruises past.*

The richly textured tapestry of an anemone forms the backdrop for a daintily spotted damselfish Dascyllus trimaculatus. ▶

There are numerous islands in the remote central portion of the Indian Ocean—Aldabra, Astove, Cosmoledo, and the Comores. When facilities are established, these isolated reefs will be more stars for divers to enjoy in years to come.

The delicate polyps of a soft coral colony bloom radiantly in utter darkness.

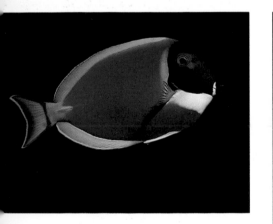

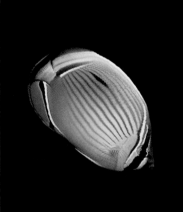

The blue tang Acanthurus leucosternon *of the Indian Ocean makes one wonder about why fish designs and colors evolve as they do.*

The butterflyfish Chaetodon trifasciata's *luminous colors stand out against the darkness of open water.*

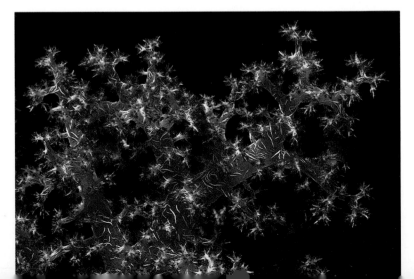

The Red Sea

*I*n the aftermath of the Gulf War this magnificent sea is emerging once again as a major destination. For two decades, divers have visited the Red Sea between wars and political crises. Throughout all these episodes the reefs have been totally unaffected by any military action; the more distant reefs are as pristine and unspoiled as ever.

It must, however, be pointed out that some of the reefs most convenient to the diving facilities in the northern Red Sea have been damaged by the unavoidable impact of thousands of divers. It is sadly true that even careful, conservation-minded divers inevitably damage reefs. Not even the richest reefs can regenerate the damage caused by daily (or even weekly) dive groups. Therefore, any potential visitor must use live-aboard boats to dive the reefs I describe here.

At their best, the reefs of the Red Sea are the equal of any in the world; the best of these gems occur as scattered islets

◀ *The shallow reefs of the Red Sea are home to countless billions of orange fairy basslets* Anthias squammipinnus.

and reef lines flung haphazardly down the center of the sea. I have taken cruises with divers on 700-mile odysseys through these distant complexes, and found reefs filled with incredibly lush life.

One's overwhelming impression here is of riotously colorful, busy, and varied marine life. Soft coral colonies in brilliant colors occur at all depths, and many can be found near the surface. Add to this tapestry vast clouds of startlingly orange fairy basslets, and mere photography is totally unable to capture what one sees. Only the mind can absorb nature's multifaceted panorama, and even the mind and its receptor senses are sometimes filled to overload.

On some coral pinnacles where currents bring generous feeding, life occurs in dense layers: hard corals form the substrate but are profusely filigreed with soft corals, gorgonian fans, and crinoids, then a layer of hovering anchovy and silversides form a swirling blanket; while above, fairy basslets dance wildly as they pluck plankton from the moving water. Sometimes the riches are so abundant that our eyes strain to isolate individual creatures to observe.

In the 1970s, such riches extended all the way north to Sharm-el-Shiekh. Then dive centers proliferated and all of the divers frequented reefs within a radius of perhaps twenty miles. Today, some of the reefs which were world famous in those days are in serious decline. Yet, outside that radius we find reefs that appear untouched; their inconvenient distance has saved them.

Typically, reefs in the Red Sea extend right to the surface. They are therefore as accessible to snorkelers as to scuba divers. From these shallow crests a reef will plunge vertically

The bannerfish Heniochus *occurs singly and in social schools of a hundred or more.*

A resting lionfish Pterois radiata. ▶

The imperial angelfish Pomacanthus imperator *is large but cautious, preferring to hide. A challenging confident pose like this is rare.*

hundreds of feet, interrupted by ledges, valleys, and shelves on the descent to depths approaching two thousand feet.

The vertical nature of these walls brings pelagic species to the coral battlements; it is not at all unusual for turtles, mantas, sharks, and barracuda to patrol these walls, pleasantly interrupting our enjoyment of smaller creatures.

At certain reef towers such as Elphinstone, Sha'ab Rumi, and Sanganeb Reef, the reef shapes resemble vast sub-

(Previous left) *Butterflyfish offer a beauty pageant of lavish color. This is a pair of* Chaetodon austriacus.

(Previous right) *Three nudibranchs* Chromodoris quadricolor *browse on a red sponge.*

The Red Sea is a rewarding arena for underwater photography. This is Chaetodon melannotus, *a shy butterflyfish.*

Rare and exciting is the butterflyfish Chaetodon larvatus.

A trademark species unique to the Red Sea is Chaetodon semilarvatus.

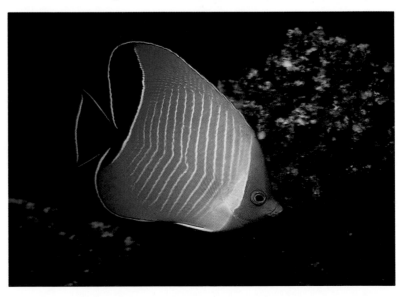

Busy harlequin wrasse Halichoeres *bustle about the reef searching for food.*

A grouper Cephalopholis miniatus *stares intently, as if trying to understand the stranger's motives.*

Resplendent in gold, a clownfish Amphiprion bicinctus *hovers above its host anemone.*

Motionless on the reef while the dainty fish pass by is the scorpionfish Scorpaenodes. *With a sudden opening of its huge mouth it will inhale the unwary.*

One of the most colorful of all reef species is Pygoplites diacanthus, *the king angelfish.*

A massive grouper Plectropoma maculatus *watches me, torn between bolting to safety or letting the cleaner wrasse finish its service.*

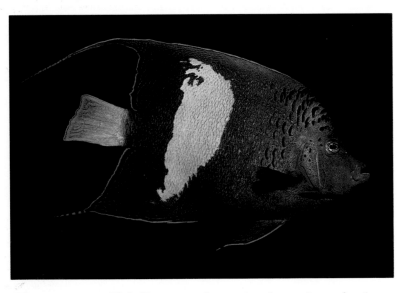

The map angelfish Pomacanthus maculatus *is endemic to the Red Sea.*

marines: the sail portion comes to the surface, but long, hull-like shelves at 60–100 feet extend far to the north and south. Schooling gray sharks and hammerheads frequent the Stygian gloom on the flanks of these deep reefs.

What qualifies these Red Sea reefs for the pantheon of divers' dreams is that they have everything: crowded shallows filled with movement and bright color, stunning vertical dropoffs, the drama of pelagic intruders appearing without warning.

There can even be drama in miniature: the shallow reefs are home to some huge, thick-bodied moray eels. When a human visitor suddenly comes face to face with a sassy specimen, it is often the human who backs off and moves on.

With luck, care, and the protection of remoteness, the best of these reefs will see limited visitors for years to come. As long as they lie beyond the horizon of most divers, the lucky few who experience them will be graced beyond measure.

After I proffer a fish carcass, two eager gray sharks Carcharrhinus amblyrhynchos *rush in to attack.*▶

Conclusion

*E*ach year sees the announcement of new, exotic diving destinations. Some of these, such as Papua New Guinea and the northern Sudan really are world-class finds, enriching our future heritage. Others are mere places, capitalizing on divers' hunger for the new and the unknown.

As we have seen, the world's great reefs qualify for that appellation by meeting certain criteria. They should have rich and varied smaller life such as corals and reef fish, the drama of plunging walls, large pelagic species to make our pulses race, and crystal clear water so we may enjoy all of these thrills to their fullest. Some enthusiasts would add sunken wrecks or other criteria to the checklist, but I consider those to be special-interest categories rather than bedrock components to measure quality.

Before you say it, of course these are subjective criteria; if one were to create a tabular score sheet different divers would score each locale differently. I might consider the shallow reef life of the Red Sea or New Guinea or the Philippines as best, but I know divers who would rate the Caribbean as highly.

◄ *Serpulid worms such as* Spirobranchus giganteus *are among the most radiant of all reef creatures.*

Even more crucial is that divers will disagree on the relative weight given to water clarity, dropoffs, coral gardens, and larger species. I personally love larger animals, so the great white sharks of south Australia, the manta rays of Yap, the hammerheads of Cocos, and the gray sharks of the Coral Sea, New Guinea, and Sudan score highly on my list.

My second most vital category would be coral gardens. Reefs endowed with fabulous color and complexity in the smaller life also get my best ratings. Here, places such as the Sudan, Philippines, New Guinea, and Fiji earn special distinction, while spectacular single dive sites such as Pixie

A placid reeftop in Fiji.

Pinnacle on the Great Barrier Reef may sparkle amid otherwise lackluster reefs.

The clear water criterion is almost a bonus category— photography benefits greatly from gin-clear water, and avoiding the speckled effect of backscatter is much easier. I must concede, however, that murky water is often foodfilled water supporting profuse marine life. One will almost always find a broader range of species and more examples of each on a reef with forty-foot visibility amid distracting plankton than in persistently clear water. The great treasure, of course, is to be at that murky site on the occasional day when it clears.

Vertical dropoffs such as those in the Cayman Islands, Red Sea, New Guinea, Micronesia, and the Coral Sea impart the sensation of space-walking to our dives. Often, the world's finest dive sites have it all—rich coral shallows in clear water at the crest of a plunging wall. Add some larger pelagics and you have the recipe for greatness.

When all is said and done, diving is a completely personal and subjective endeavor. I would not presume to say that my criteria are *the* criteria; instead I have presented a personal chronicle of two decades on the world's premiere reefs. The chronicle is not over—there are a number of world-class sites that presently have no diving access, or that I have not been fortunate enough to experience as yet. The voyage of discovery continues.

Do I have my own personal favorites? Of course, and they are favorites because of my personal experiences there. I do, however, know that others will react to them differently. I once took a nudibranch enthusiast to what I thought was one of the world's finest reefs. He was bitterly disappointed because despite all its greatness in other ways it was deficient in nudibranchs. So it goes.

◄ *A sunset heralds the end of our adventures.*

In a graceful farewell, a manta ray Manta birostris *soars against the sun.*

Each of you will choose and judge as you travel the world's tropics. Under the glinting surface of those tropic seas you will render your judgments.

I hope when you dive that you will both savor and protect the treasure you experience. When you dive, try to select your handholds only of dead coral; don't destroy creatures with careless fin-strokes. Don't chase marine creatures and frighten them.

On the larger stage, I urge you to support sane rather than extremist conservation policy, to preserve the best possible environment for all creatures, including humans.

May your own voyage of discovery be filled with wonder; may the reefs of the blue planet reveal their hidden treasure to you; may the creatures of the sea open their secret hearts to you and give you peace . . .

Index

Numbers in bold indicate photograph.